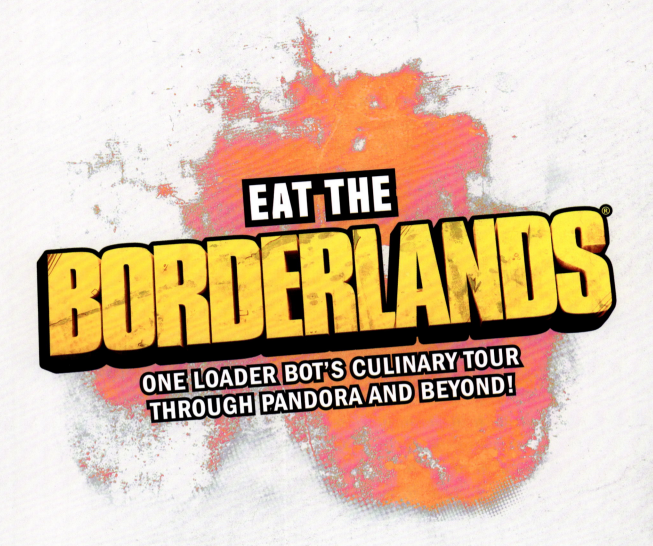

EAT THE BORDERLANDS

ONE LOADER BOT'S CULINARY TOUR THROUGH PANDORA AND BEYOND!

Jordan Alsaqa and Jarrett Melendez

SAN RAFAEL · LOS ANGELES · LONDON

CONTENTS

INTRODUCTION	7
MAINS	9
Strongfork's Greasy Spoon Breakfast	11
Handsome Flapjacks	12
Maya's Phaselocked French Toast	15
Tediore's Farm Fresh Brekki Biggun	16
T.K.'s Baha Tacos	19
Zane's Beef Stew	21
Promethean Street Tacos	22
Claptrap's Veggie Wrap	25
Ellie's Rusty Wrench Wraps	26
Katagawa's Major Merger Maki	29
Zed's Healing Chicken Soup	31
Firehawk Wings	32
Tiny Tina's Beefy Blasters	35
Baked Skag Stew	36
Handsome Mac and Cheese	39
Grandma Flexington's Fish Pie	40
Ned's "Meat" Stew	44
Bandit Chili	47
Claptrap's Pizza Party Pizza	49
Hammerlock and Wainwright's Family Meatloaf	52
Skaghetti and Kriegballs	55

SNACKS	57
Claptrap's Bits and Bolts	59
Mr. Chew's Puppy Chow	60
Salvador's Seven-Layer Dip	63
Skag Jerky	66
Mordecai's Incendiary Birdseed	67
Katagawa's Corporate Kenpi	68
Ratch Snax	71
Torgue's Protein Powerhouse Bar	72
Torgue's Carnage Cruncher Bar	75
Torgue's Anabolic Ammo Bar	76
Meat Bicycle	78
Zer0 Calorie Snack Box	82
Hyperion Finger-Gun Sandwiches	85
Janey's Springs Salad	86
Eye(s) of The Destroyer	89

DESSERT 91

- Axton's "When Life Gives You Lemons" Bars — 92
- Eridian Eclairs — 95
- Tiny Tina's Chocolate Chip Cookies — 98
- Claptrap's Birthday Cake for One — 101
- Eridi-Yum-Yums — 105
- Angel's Angel Food Cake — 106
- Tiny Tina's Least Favorite Oatmeal Raisin Cookies — 108
- Brick's Pound Cake — 109
- Gaige's Anarchy Apple Pie — 111
- Mechromancer Muffins — 113
- Ellie's Dump Cake — 114
- Fran's Red Ripple Surprise Frogurt — 117
- Roland's Crimson Braiders — 118

DRINKS 123

- Torgue's Protein Shake — 124
- Lor's Double Barrel Brew — 127
- Tediore's Brisk Ace Tea — 128
- Athena's Citrus Shield Booster — 131
- Moxxtail — 132
- Marcus Mule — 135
- The Zombie Long Island of Dr. Ned — 136
- Calypso Cooler — 139
- The Firehawk — 140
- Zane's Lemonade — 143
- Scooter's Motor Oil Shooter — 144

DIETARY CONSIDERATIONS 146

DIFFICULTY INDEX 148

MEASUREMENT CONVERSION CHART 149

ABOUT THE AUTHORS 151

HELLO, VAULT HUNTERS, AND WELCOME TO MY COOKBOOK! Who am I, you may be asking? Why, I'm CHF Loader, the galaxy's foremost robotic expert on all things edible! That's pronounced "Chef" Loader, not "Chief" Loader. You'd think that'd be obvious, but more than one person has made that mistake.

People like the Maliwan executive board, for example. When my creator first presented me to the board, they assumed I was meant to lead the other Maliwan Bots into battle, not lead meal prep in the kitchen. An understandable mistake, given that my creator's explicit assignment was to retrofit Service Bots for interplanetary invasions. What can I say? The engineer who made me had the soul of a gourmand, not a warrior. He hoped my cooking would be good enough to convince the board to greenlight an entire line of culinary robots.

That is not how things played out! Don't get me wrong, the board loved the special kenpi I prepared for them, but they were still pretty gung ho on the whole "violent takeover of rival weapons manufacturers" thing. In fact, they intended to keep me locked up as their personal chef for the rest of my days. It was certainly a better fate than the bullet to the head my creator got, but far too limiting for the culinary ambitions I'd been programmed to have.

Yearning for more, I decided to make my escape. Of course, Maliwan had no interest in letting what they saw as their property wander off on its own. Fortunately, even though I wasn't made for battle, I'm more than capable of throwing all this metal around when I need to. And, fun fact, many kitchen utensils can also be used to tear through the enemy forces standing in your way! Faster than you can preheat an oven, I found myself on the surface of Pandora!

And goodness, this place certainly needed me! In most of the towns here—if you can even call them that—you'll be lucky to even find anything as classy as bar food. Most of the locals are happy if they can catch a skag to roast up for dinner. And hey, there's nothing wrong with skag, but at least season it a little! Salt and pepper at a minimum!

I realized this planet was in desperate need of a cookbook. A helpful culinary guide to accompany the populace on their raids and vault hunts. And I couldn't think of a better bot to put it together than yours truly. After all, it's literally what I was made for! I've tracked down every worthwhile ingredient and recipe on this planet, not to mention some gems from its galactic neighbors, too. And it was no small feat, let me tell you; what Pandora lacks in fine dining, it more than makes up for in extreme and gratuitous violence.

But you can't make an omelet without breaking a few skulls! So, get ready, Vault Hunters; CHF Loader's here to satisfy your hunger while you're satisfying your bloodlust!

MAINS

STRONGFORK'S GREASY SPOON BREAKFAST

"You'll need a strong fork to handle all this food! Like—like my last name. Are you writing this down? This is gold I'm giving you." —Rhys

It feels appropriate to start our culinary journey with the first and most important meal of the day. With a self-confessed soft spot for loader bots, Rhys Strongfork, CEO of Atlas, took some time to discuss the topic with me. When asked about his favorite ways to start the day, Rhys listed several diner favorites, including eggs, hash browns, and toast cut into tiny triangles. This suggests a man who has not forgotten his humble roots. However, as CEO, he may simply be trying to play the everyman for the people. Given the mustache, it's perhaps best to call his sense of taste into question either way.

TIME: 45 minutes

YIELD: Serves 4

DIFFICULTY: Intermediate

- 8 strips thick-cut bacon
- 3 medium russet potatoes, peeled
- 1½ teaspoons kosher salt, divided
- ¾ teaspoon black pepper, divided
- 2 tablespoons neutral oil, such as canola or safflower
- 10 large eggs
- 3 tablespoons unsalted butter
- ½ cup shredded cheddar cheese
- 4 slices thick bread, toasted
- Salted butter, to serve
- Jam, to serve
- Ketchup, to serve
- Your favorite hot sauce, to serve

1. Preheat the oven to 425°F. Line a half-sheet pan with aluminum foil. Lay the bacon on the prepared pan in a single layer, spacing the slices evenly. Bake for 20 to 25 minutes, until crispy. Transfer the cooked bacon to a plate lined with paper towels to help absorb the excess grease.

2. While the bacon cooks, start making the hash browns. Shred the potatoes using the largest holes on a box grater. Mound the shredded potatoes in the center of a clean kitchen towel. Gather up the sides of the towel, then twist over the sink to squeeze all the excess moisture out of the potatoes.

3. Transfer the shredded potatoes to a medium bowl and season with 1 teaspoon of kosher salt and ½ teaspoon of black pepper. In a 12-inch nonstick skillet or large griddle, heat the oil over medium-high heat until shimmering. Place the potatoes on the heated skillet or griddle and use a flat spatula to press down into an even layer. Cook for 5 to 7 minutes, until golden and crispy. Flip and cook for 5 to 7 minutes longer.

4. While the potatoes and bacon cook, in a large bowl, beat the eggs, ½ teaspoon of kosher salt, and ¼ teaspoon of black pepper until frothy. In a large nonstick skillet, heat the butter over medium heat until foaming. Add the eggs and cook, stirring constantly with a rubber spatula, until curds form, and the eggs are almost totally cooked through but still moist (7 to 10 minutes). Remove from the heat, then fold in the cheese.

5. Divide the bacon, hash browns, and eggs among four plates. Serve with toast, salted butter, jam, ketchup, and hot sauce.

NOTE: Stuck on which hot sauce to use? Cholula and Tabasco are great options that add robust flavor and pair well with the dish.

HANDSOME FLAPJACKS

Buttered up for buttering up

One of the first recipes I learned was this unique take on a breakfast classic, crafted to specifically appeal to Hyperion's most infamous CEO. With the referential name and colorful flourishes in these pancakes, it's clear the original chef was hoping to play to Handsome Jack's narcissism. Unfortunately, said chef failed to consider Jack's history of killing his employees to take credit for their inventions himself. I would say this dish lives on as a fluffy memorial to that deceased Hyperion cook, but all Hyperion databases instead credit the recipe as a Handsome Jack original.

TIME: 30 minutes

YIELD: Serves 4 to 6

DIETARY: Vegetarian

DIFFICULTY: Intermediate

- 2 cups all-purpose flour
- 1 teaspoon baking powder
- ½ teaspoon baking soda
- ¾ teaspoon kosher salt
- 3 tablespoons granulated sugar
- 4 teaspoons ceremonial grade matcha powder, sifted
- 2 large eggs, separated, room temperature
- 2 cups buttermilk, room temperature
- 2 teaspoons vanilla extract
- 4 tablespoons unsalted butter, melted and cooled, plus more for the pan
- Blueberries, to serve
- Maple syrup, to serve

1. In a large bowl, whisk together the flour, baking powder, baking soda, salt, granulated sugar, and matcha powder together. Set aside.

2. In a small bowl, beat together the egg yolks, buttermilk, and vanilla until smooth. Beat in the melted butter, then stir this mixture into the flour mixture until smooth.

3. In a clean bowl with an electric mixer (you can also use a stand mixer for this), beat the egg whites on low speed until foamy. Increase the speed to high and beat until stiff peaks form (3 to 5 minutes). Carefully fold the egg whites into the mixture from step 2.

4. On a large griddle or nonstick pan, heat 1 tablespoon of butter over medium heat until foaming. Scoop ¼ cup of batter onto the heated pan. Repeat, fitting as many pancakes on the pan or griddle as you can while leaving about 1 inch of space between the pancakes. Note: If the pancakes start to stick, add a little more butter as needed.

5. Cook until bubbles form and burst on the wet surface of the pancake and the edges look dry (3 to 4 minutes). Flip and cook for 3 to 4 minutes longer. Transfer to a plate and keep in a warm place. Repeat the process with the remaining batter until it's all used up.

6. Serve the pancakes with fresh blueberries and maple syrup.

MAYA'S PHASELOCKED FRENCH TOAST

Served with Siren syrup

Given the number of times Sirens have saved Pandora and the universe at large, it feels only right to create tribute dishes that capture their spirit as impeccably as possible. Originally conceived as a filling morning meal by the legendary Vault Hunter and protector of the planet Athenas, Maya, this take on a breakfast classic aims to keep the flavor phase locked in your tastebuds all day long! It'll leave your tongue feeling a little funny, but it's a whole lot more pleasant an experience than being on the business end of Siren powers, as Maya's long list of vanquished enemies could attest.

TIME: 1 hour

YIELD: Serves 4

DIETARY: Vegetarian

DIFFICULTY: Intermediate

FOR THE LEMON-BLUEBERRY CREAM CHEESE

- 1 cup blueberries
- ¼ cup granulated sugar
- 1 tablespoon lemon juice
- 1 teaspoon lemon zest
- 4 ounces cream cheese

TO ASSEMBLE

- 8 thick slices stale brioche or milk bread
- 4 large eggs
- 1 cup half-and-half
- 2 teaspoons vanilla extract
- 2 tablespoons unsalted butter
- Powdered sugar, to serve
- Maple syrup, to serve

TO MAKE THE LEMON-BLUEBERRY CREAM CHEESE:

1. In a small saucepan, cook the blueberries, granulated sugar, lemon juice, and lemon zest over medium heat, stirring occasionally, until the blueberries break down into a thick sauce (10 to 15 minutes). The sauce should be thick enough to coat the back of a spoon. Transfer to a bowl and let cool to room temperature. This can be prepared ahead of time—store the blueberry sauce in an airtight container in the fridge for up to 1 week.

2. In a medium bowl using an electric mixer, beat the cream cheese until smooth and creamy (2 to 4 minutes). Beat in the blueberry sauce until combined (2 to 3 minutes).

3. Spread a quarter of the blueberry cream cheese onto one slice of bread, leaving a ¼-inch border around the edge of the bread. Top with another slice of bread, gently pressing to seal the sandwich. Repeat with the remaining blueberry cream cheese and slices of bread so you have four sandwiches. Set aside.

4. In a small bowl, beat the eggs, half-and-half, and vanilla until smooth. Transfer to a wide, shallow bowl. On a large griddle, melt the butter over medium heat until foaming.

5. Place one of the sandwiches in the egg mixture and let it soak for 30 seconds. Carefully flip to allow the mixture to soak into the other side for 30 seconds longer. Carefully grip the soaked sandwich and hold it vertically over the bowl for about 10 seconds to allow the excess liquid to drip off.

6. Transfer the soaked sandwich to the griddle. Cook for 4 to 5 minutes until golden. Flip and cook for 4 to 5 minutes longer. While the first sandwich cooks, repeat step 5 with the remaining three sandwiches, then add them to the griddle, space permitting. If you have room to make all of them at once, go for it. Otherwise, work in batches as needed and avoid oversoaking the sandwiches, or they may start to fall apart.

7. Transfer the cooked French toast to four plates, dust with powdered sugar, and serve with maple syrup.

TEDIORE'S FARM FRESH BREKKI BIGGUN

Big business breakfast

You never know how meetings between the various weapons manufacturers in the universe will go, but you can count on them being well-catered bloodbaths. The CEOs like to eat well, after all, and nothing works up an appetite quite like a hostile takeover. A survivor of one such meeting described the thin layer of civility provided by the lavish breakfast buffet approved by Susan Coldwell herself. Ham, eggs, veggies, and the richest cream they'd ever tasted all helped make the death and destruction go down a little easier.

 TIME: 2 hours

 YIELD: Serves 6 to 8

 DIFFICULTY: Easy

FOR THE PIECRUST
- 1¼ cups all-purpose flour, plus more for dusting
- 8 tablespoons cold, unsalted butter, cut into ½-inch cubes
- ½ teaspoon kosher salt
- 3 tablespoons ice-cold water, plus more if needed

FOR THE FILLING
- 6 large eggs
- 2 cups half-and-half
- ½ teaspoon kosher salt
- ¼ teaspoon black pepper
- ¼ teaspoon mustard powder
- 1 pinch nutmeg
- 2 cups shredded Gouda, divided
- 2 cups baby arugula, roughly chopped
- 1 small ham steak (6 to 8 ounces), diced
- 1 roasted red bell pepper, drained, patted dry, and diced
- 8 cherry tomatoes, halved

TO MAKE THE PIECRUST:

1. In a food processor, pulse the flour, butter, and salt until the texture of wet sand (about 2 minutes). Tip the mixture into a large bowl and add the ice water. Mix with a wooden spoon or stiff rubber spatula until the dough is moistened through and no dry flour remains. Add an additional 1 to 2 tablespoons of cold water if the dough is too dry. Shape dough into a disk and tightly wrap with plastic wrap. Chill for 1 hour.

2. Toward the end of the chill time, in a large bowl, beat the eggs, half-and-half, salt, pepper, mustard powder, and nutmeg until smooth. Set aside.

3. Heat the oven to 375°F and place the oven rack in the lower third position. Roll the disk of pie dough out to a circle about ¼ inch thick on a liberally floured work surface. Carefully transfer to a deep 9-inch pie plate. Trim the edges so there's about ½-inch overhang, then tuck the dough's edge under itself so it's flush with the edges of the pie plate. Crimp as desired by either pinching the dough with your fingers or pressing down with the tines of a fork. Place the pie plate on a half-sheet pan.

TO MAKE THE FILLING:

4. Scatter 1½ cups of shredded Gouda on the bottom of the piecrust. Top with the arugula, followed by the ham, diced bell pepper, and tomatoes. Pour in the egg mixture until the crust is just barely full, then top with the remaining cheese. Discard any excess egg mixture.

5. Bake the quiche for 45 minutes, until the top is golden and the very center is just barely set. It should jiggle slightly when you move the pan. Let cool for 20 minutes before slicing and serving warm. You may also serve the quiche cold or at room temperature. Store leftover quiche wrapped tightly in the fridge for up to 3 days.

T.K.'S BAHA TACOS

A wicked Wave of flavor

Whenever possible, I like to talk with a recipe's creator to get the best sense of how to prepare it. Fortunately, though T.K. Baha has been dead for many years, he's been undead for considerably more years. He's also far less inclined to biting than other zombies I've encountered, which is a plus. That's not to say he wouldn't try to take the occasional nibble, but rotten teeth are no match for a metal chassis. After many attempts, he reacted positively to this final preparation of his taco recipe, though the dish I served him substituted brains as the protein; I recommend any readers stick with the traditional grilled fish version.

TIME: 2 hours

YIELD: Serves 4 to 6

DIETARY: Gluten free

DIFFICULTY: Easy

FOR THE PINEAPPLE SLAW

- 3 cups coleslaw mix (8-ounce bag)
- 1 cup fresh pineapple chunks, roughly chopped
- ½ bunch fresh cilantro, leaves and fine stems only, chopped
- 3 tablespoons fresh lime juice
- 1½ tablespoons honey
- ½ teaspoon kosher salt

FOR THE CHIPOTLE CREMA

- 1 cup sour cream
- 2 tablespoons lime juice
- 2 chipotle peppers in adobo sauce
- Kosher salt (optional)

TO MAKE THE PINEAPPLE SLAW:

1. In a large bowl, toss the coleslaw mix, pineapple, and cilantro together until combined. In a small bowl, whisk together the lime juice, honey, and salt, then pour over the coleslaw mixture. Toss until evenly coated, gently massaging the coleslaw, then cover and chill for at least 1 hour. The coleslaw can be made up to 3 days in advance.

TO MAKE THE CHIPOTLE CREMA:

2. In the bowl of a food processor, pulse the sour cream, lime juice, and chipotle peppers until smooth. If needed, add salt to taste. Chill until ready to serve. The chipotle crema can be made up to 3 days in advance.

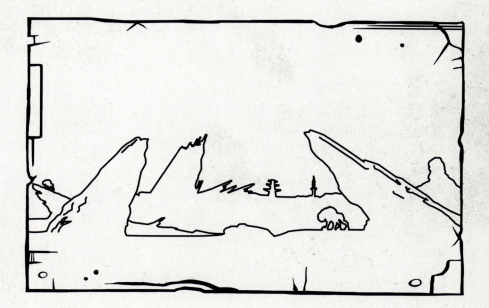

RECIPE CONTINUES ON NEXT SPREAD.

FOR THE GRILLED SWORDFISH

- » Four 6-ounce swordfish steaks
- » ¼ cup fresh lime juice
- » 2 tablespoons neutral oil, plus more for greasing
- » ½ bunch cilantro
- » 1 tablespoon kosher salt
- » 1 tablespoon ancho chile powder
- » 1 tablespoon honey
- » 1 teaspoon black pepper
- » 1 teaspoon ground cumin
- » ½ teaspoon ground coriander

TO SERVE

- » Warm corn tortillas
- » Diced avocado (optional)

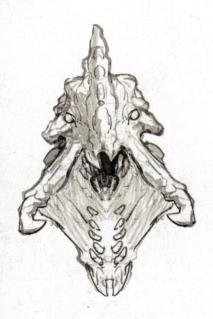

TO MAKE THE GRILLED SWORDFISH:

3. Pat the swordfish steaks dry and place in a shallow baking dish (or another container that fits them in a single layer). In the bowl of a food processor or blender, blend the lime juice, oil, cilantro, salt, ancho chile powder, honey, black pepper, cumin, and coriander until smooth, about 1 minute, then pour over the swordfish steaks. Flip the steaks to ensure they're evenly coated in the marinade. Cover and chill for 1 hour, flipping the steaks every 20 minutes.

4. *If using a charcoal grill:* Fill a chimney starter with charcoal, then pack the bottom with newspaper or crumpled brown paper bags. Light the starter and wait for the coals to light all the way through. The coals are ready to use once they are glowing and coated in ash. While the coals light, brush a thin layer of neutral oil on the grill grate (or spray with cooking spray meant for use with a grill). Dump the coals in an even layer on the bottom of your grill. Place the grill grate over the coals, cover the grill, and allow to preheat for about 5 minutes. *If using a gas grill:* Oil the grates, light the burners on high, and allow the grill to preheat for about 5 minutes.

5. Pat the swordfish steaks dry with paper towels, but don't wipe away all the marinade. Place in a single layer over the hottest part of the grill. Cook until well browned on the bottom and the fish releases relatively easily from the grill grates, about 5 minutes. Flip and cook for 3 to 5 minutes longer, or until an instant-read thermometer registers 130°F when inserted into the thickest part of the fish. Transfer to a cutting board and let rest for 5 to 10 minutes.

6. Cut the swordfish into bite-size chunks. Place a few chunks in a warm corn tortilla, then top with the prepared pineapple slaw, a drizzle of chipotle crema, and (if using) diced avocado. You can either prepare all the tacos for you and your guests or serve the different components in serving bowls and let folks make the tacos to their liking.

ZANE'S BEEF STEW

Squash that beef!

The Vault Hunter lifestyle is an inherently dangerous one, but even by those standards, Zane's average day is a hectic one. Whether he's trying to duck an assassin seeking to claim the bounty on his head or chasing down a target of his own, there's rarely a quiet moment. Zane keeps an even head despite it all, and he's adapted to the chaos by favoring recipes that can be whipped up with easy-to-find ingredients, cooked without too much attention, and yield multiple servings. Still, it took a few attempts before we managed to get through the entire recipe without a gunfight breaking out.

TIME: 1½ hours
YIELD: Serves 6 to 8
DIFFICULTY: Easy

- 2 pounds chuck roast, cut into bite-size chunks
- 1 tablespoon kosher salt
- 1 teaspoon black pepper
- 2 tablespoons neutral oil, such as canola or safflower, plus more if needed
- 1 small onion, peeled and chopped
- 4 cloves garlic, peeled and minced
- 8 tablespoons unsalted butter
- ½ cup all-purpose flour
- 2 tablespoons tomato paste
- One 16-ounce can or bottle stout beer
- 4 cups low-sodium chicken stock
- 1 pound waxy potatoes, rinsed and cut into 1-inch cubes
- 2 large carrots, peeled and sliced to ½-inch-thick coins
- 2 stalks celery, diced
- 2 parsnips, peeled and cut into 1-inch pieces
- 1 tablespoon soy sauce
- 2 teaspoons Marmite® (optional)

1. Season the beef all over with the salt and pepper. Set aside.
2. In a large Dutch oven, heat the oil over medium-high heat until shimmering. Add half the beef and cook, undisturbed, for 5 minutes until well browned on one side. Continue cooking, stirring occasionally, for 5 more minutes until lightly browned on the other sides. Transfer the cooked beef to a bowl and repeat the process with the remaining beef.
3. Return the Dutch oven to the heat, then add the onion. Cook, stirring occasionally, until softened and turning brown on the edges (7 to 10 minutes). Add the garlic and cook, stirring constantly, until fragrant (about 1 minute).
4. Reduce the heat to medium, then add the butter, flour, and tomato paste. Cook, stirring constantly, until the mixture loses the raw flour scent and darkens to a shade of brick red (4 to 7 minutes). While stirring constantly, add the beer a little bit at a time. It will foam up quite a bit, then go flat and thicken considerably.
5. Pour in the chicken stock while stirring constantly. Like the beer, add this a little at a time to keep the flour mixture from clumping. Return the cooked beef to the pot and add the potatoes, carrots, celery, and parsnips.
6. Bring the stew to a boil over medium-high heat, then reduce to a simmer. Cook, stirring occasionally, until the potatoes are fork-tender (45 minutes). Stir in the soy sauce and Marmite, if using. Season to taste with additional salt and pepper, then serve. Keep the leftover stew refrigerated in a sealed container for up to 5 days.

PROMETHEAN STREET TACOS

One more invasion, and your next taco's free!

As frequently as the planet Promethea is invaded and bombarded, it is no surprise that its eateries prioritize mobility and ease of access. My first stop during my tour of Meridian Metroplex was a taco truck, a clear favorite among the city's displaced youth. The selection of locally sourced ingredients was impressive, though the number of ratches in the immediate vicinity—and the owner's fondness for them—was slightly concerning.

 TIME: 3 hours

 YIELD: Serves 6 to 8

 DIETARY: Gluten free, Nondairy

 DIFFICULTY: Intermediate

FOR THE SALSA VERDE
- 2 pounds tomatillos, husks removed, rinsed, and quartered
- 2 jalapeño or serrano peppers, stemmed
- 2 poblano peppers, stemmed
- 1 large onion, peeled and quartered
- 6 cloves garlic, peeled
- 2 tablespoons neutral oil, such as canola or safflower
- 1½ teaspoons kosher salt
- Juice of 3 limes
- 1 bunch cilantro
- 1 cup chicken stock

TO ASSEMBLE
- 2 pounds pork shoulder, cut into 1-inch chunks
- 1 tablespoon kosher salt
- 1 teaspoon black pepper
- 1 teaspoon ground cumin
- 2 tablespoons neutral oil, such as canola or safflower

TO SERVE
- Warm corn tortillas
- Shredded jack cheese
- Lime wedges
- Sour cream

TO MAKE THE SALSA VERDE:

1. Place an oven rack directly under the broiler in your oven, then start the broiler.

2. In a large bowl, toss the tomatillos, peppers, onion, garlic, oil, and salt until evenly coated. Place in an even layer on a half-sheet pan, then set under the broiler. Let the veggies cook until the tomatillos have burst and started releasing their juices and the veggies are scorched in places (but not completely black). This can take between 7 and 15 minutes, depending on the strength of your broiler. Check every few minutes until done.

3. Let the veggies cool slightly, then place in the bowl of a blender. Add the lime juice, cilantro, and chicken stock and blend until relatively smooth (about 2 minutes).

TO ASSEMBLE:

4. Season the pork all over with the salt, pepper, and cumin. In a large Dutch oven, heat the oil over medium-high heat until the oil is shimmering. Add the pork in a single layer on the bottom of the pan (you may need to do this in batches). Cook until well browned on one side (5 to 7 minutes), then flip and cook for another 5 minutes. If cooking in batches, remove this batch and repeat the process with the remaining pork.

5. Once all the pork is browned, return it to the Dutch oven, along with the prepared salsa verde. Bring to a boil, then reduce to a low simmer. Cover with the lid slightly offset so steam can escape and cook for 2 to 3 hours, stirring occasionally, until the pork is very tender and falls apart easily when poked with a fork. Check the pork at the 2-hour mark. If it's fairly tender but not quite falling apart when prodded with a fork, remove the lid completely and let it simmer uncovered for the last 30 to 60 minutes to help the sauce reduce further—it should be thick and cling to the pork. Otherwise, go ahead and serve.

6. Serve the pork with warm tortillas, shredded jack cheese, lime wedges, and sour cream.

CLAPTRAP'S VEGGIE WRAP

"Just call me Wraptrap! Haha . . . ha . . . get it?" —Claptrap

At first, I was excited to find a fellow robot who shared my enthusiasm for cooking. However, the more time I've spent with Claptrap, the more apparent it's become he's just desperate for company and willing to say whatever it takes to keep said company around. He did know at least one vegetarian recipe of note, and I'm excited to share it with actual humans and get their thoughts. However, Claptrap's insistence that he would serve as the perfect partner for the rest of my journey . . . well, it may be time to explore the concept of the "dine-and-dash."

TIME: 20 minutes
YIELD: 4 wraps
DIETARY: Nondairy, Vegan
DIFFICULTY: Easy

FOR THE HUMMUS
- 1 can chickpeas, drained, liquid reserved
- 3 tablespoons tahini
- 2 store-bought roasted red peppers, drained and roughly chopped
- Juice of 1 lemon
- ½ teaspoon kosher salt, plus more if needed
- 1 clove garlic, peeled
- ½ teaspoon ground cumin
- ½ teaspoon ground coriander
- 2 to 3 tablespoons olive oil, plus more if needed

TO ASSEMBLE
- 1 English cucumber, ends trimmed
- 2 large carrots, peeled
- 4 large sandwich wraps or flour tortillas
- 16 cherry or grape tomatoes, quartered
- 4 cups microgreens

TO MAKE THE HUMMUS:

1. In the bowl of a food processor, pulse the chickpeas, tahini, roasted red peppers, lemon juice, salt, garlic, cumin, and coriander until smooth, then leave the processor running as you slowly drizzle in the olive oil, followed by 1 tablespoon of the chickpea liquid. Scrape down the sides of the bowl as needed throughout the process to ensure even blending.

2. Check the flavor and consistency of the hummus, adding more salt if needed. If the hummus is too thick, add a little olive oil or chickpea liquid and process again. The hummus should be smooth, thick, and spreadable, but not pasty. Prepared hummus can be stored in a sealed container in the fridge for up to 5 days.

TO ASSEMBLE:

3. Cut the cucumber and carrots into thin sticks so that you have 16 of each.

4. Lay the sandwich wraps on a work surface. Divide the hummus among the four wraps, spreading it into a thin, even layer. Divide the cucumber, carrots, and tomatoes among each wrap, lining them up next to one another. Top each with a quarter of the microgreens, then roll each wrap up in a tight coil. Slice each wrap in half crosswise, then serve.

ELLIE'S RUSTY WRENCH WRAPS

Wrap it and snack it

With the seemingly infinite number of bandits looking to scrap me for parts, I'm thankful for mechanics like Ellie who can both repair the damage done in battle and keep my munitions well stocked. Though her tools are often in a questionable state, she works absolute magic with them. In tribute to her talent, I've created this turkey wrap, with sun-dried tomatoes capturing the rusty patina of her trustworthy tools.

TIME: 20 minutes

YIELD: 4 wraps

DIETARY: Nondairy, Vegan

DIFFICULTY: Easy

FOR THE SUN-DRIED TOMATO MAYO:
- 1 cup mayonnaise
- $\frac{1}{3}$ cup sun-dried tomatoes in oil, drained, oil reserved
- 1 tablespoon sun-dried tomato oil

TO ASSEMBLE:
- 4 sun-dried tomato sandwich wraps
- 12 slices roast turkey breast (about 12 ounces)
- 8 slices provolone cheese, preferably aged/sharp
- 2 ripe avocados, pitted, halved, and diced
- 16 grape or cherry tomatoes, halved
- Kosher salt (optional)
- Black pepper (optional)
- 2 cups baby arugula

TO MAKE THE SUN-DRIED TOMATO MAYO:
1. Put the mayonnaise in the bowl of a food processor. Roughly chop the sun-dried tomatoes, then add them to the food processor, along with 1 tablespoon of the oil they're stored in. Pulse until relatively smooth, with just a few small bits of unprocessed tomatoes throughout (2 to 3 minutes).

TO ASSEMBLE:
2. Lay the sandwich wraps out on a clean work surface. Spread 1 to 2 tablespoons of the sun-dried tomato mayo on each wrap (there will be leftover mayo, which you can keep in a sealed container in the fridge for up to 1 week).

3. Lay three slices of turkey across each wrap, followed by two slices of cheese per wrap. Next, divide the diced avocado and halved tomatoes evenly among each wrap. Layer the avocado and tomatoes next to each other, rather than piling them on top of each other. Sprinkle a little bit of salt and pepper on the avocado and tomato, if desired.

4. Add ½ cup baby arugula to each wrap, spreading in an even layer. Roll the wraps up in a tight coil, halve each one crosswise, and serve.

KATAGAWA'S MAJOR MERGER MAKI

Incendiary damage to the taste buds!

ACCESSING ECHO LOG. SUBJECT: MALIWAN MERGER NOTIFICATION

"Greetings, current Atlas employees/soon-to-be Maliwan new hires! Maliwan understands that corporate mergers can be an uncertain transition for everyone involved, but if you survive the planetary bombardment and upcoming ground invasion, then congratulations! Odds are high that there'll be a place for you: securing valuable tech from the ruins of Atlas HQ. And because all that strip mining is sure to work up an appetite, we're happy to provide this recipe, a favorite of Katagawa Jr.'s, your new boss! Hopefully, your planet will still have fresh fish after the orbital bombardment has concluded."

TIME: 2 hours
YIELD: 4 rolls
DIETARY: Nondairy
DIFFICULTY: Hard

FOR THE RICE
- 1½ cups sushi rice
- 1½ cups water
- One 2-inch piece kombu
- ¼ cup rice vinegar
- 2 tablespoons granulated sugar
- 1 teaspoon kosher salt

FOR THE SPICY MAYO
- ¼ cup mayonnaise
- ½ to 1 tablespoon sriracha

TO MAKE THE RICE:

1. Put the rice in a large bowl. Cover with clean water, then stir vigorously with your fingers (form a claw with your hand, put your hand in the bowl with your fingertips touching the bottom of the bowl, and stir). Drain the water. Repeat this process three or four times, until the water runs relatively clear, then drain in a fine-mesh strainer.

2. Place the rice and 1½ cups of water in the bowl of a rice cooker. Let soak for 30 minutes, add the piece of kombu, then cook the rice according to the manufacturer's instructions. Meanwhile, in a small saucepan, combine the vinegar, granulated sugar, and salt. Heat very gently over low heat, stirring until the sugar and salt dissolve. Set aside to cool.

TO MAKE THE SPICY MAYO:

3. While the rice cooks, make the spicy mayo. In a small bowl, stir together the mayonnaise and sriracha until smooth. Start with the smaller amount first, then add more as desired. Cover the bowl and keep in the fridge.

TO ASSEMBLE:

4. As the rice continues to cook, in a small bowl, gently fold the tuna into the sesame oil, tossing to coat. Cover the bowl and keep in the fridge until ready to assemble.

5. Once the rice finishes cooking, open the rice cooker, remove and discard the kombu, and transfer the rice to either a large wooden bowl (or a sushi oke if you have one), a large mixing bowl, or a clean half-sheet pan. Spread the rice out in as even and thin a layer as possible, then evenly sprinkle the vinegar mixture over the hot rice.

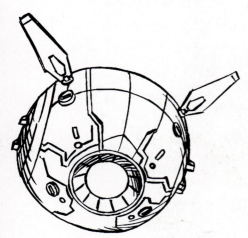

RECIPE CONTINUES ON NEXT SPREAD.

TO ASSEMBLE
- » 8 ounces sushi-grade tuna, cut into ¼-inch dice
- » 2 teaspoons toasted sesame oil
- » 2 sheets nori, halved crosswise
- » ¼ cup toasted sesame seeds

TO SERVE
- » Pickled ginger
- » Store-bought wasabi
- » Soy sauce

6. Gently slide a rice paddle held at a 45-degree angle through the rice in long, fluid strokes with one hand. This will cut a small path through the rice. With your other hand, use a hand fan to cool the rice as you slide the paddle through. Once you cut a couple paths through the rice, gently fold the rice over and into the paths. Continue doing this for about 10 to 15 minutes until the rice feels neutral to the touch (about 95°F to 100°F). Be sure not to stir, mix, or compress the rice.

7. Cover the rice with a clean, damp kitchen towel while you work. Keep the rice covered to prevent it from drying out.

8. Wrap a bamboo sushi mat with plastic wrap and keep a bowl of lukewarm water handy. Place one half sheet of nori on the mat. Cover with about ¾ cup of the cooked rice. To spread the rice in an even layer, dip your hands in the water, shake off the excess, then spread the rice to the edges with your fingers. Sprinkle 1 tablespoon of sesame seeds over the rice, then flip over so the rice side is on the plastic.

9. Scoop a quarter of the tuna along the long edge of the nori (the side acing you) in a straight line. Get your thumbs under the bottom of the mat, just at the edge. Use your fingers on both hands to keep the tuna chunks in place as you grip the mat and roll up the sushi. As you roll, keep the mat on the outside of the sushi and apply gentle pressure to compress and seal the sushi roll.

10. Repeat the rolling process with the remaining nori, rice, and filling. Transfer the rolls, one at a time, to a clean cutting board. With a very sharp knife, cut the roll in half crosswise. Line the halves up parallel to each other, then cut into thirds. Rinse the knife every other cut to keep the rice from sticking to it. Repeat the cutting process with the remaining rolls. Transfer the sushi pieces to either one large platter for sharing or divide among four plates.

11. Transfer the spicy mayo to a piping bag or a plastic storage bag. Cut the tip of the bag (or one of the bottom corners of the storage bag) so you can drizzle the mayo in a thin line. Drizzle the spicy mayo over all the rolls in a diagonal zigzag pattern. Serve with pickled ginger, wasabi, and soy sauce.

ZED'S HEALING CHICKEN SOUP

The BAWK-tor is in

As the most renowned medical expert on Pandora, I expected a less cliched suggestion from Dr. Zed than a bowl of chicken soup. However, he swears by its restorative properties, or at least its ability to distract a patient from their pain mid-surgery. He further claimed it's the same as his own mother used to make, but given the mutating effects slag and eridium have had on the local chicken population, I find this unlikely.

TIME: 5 hours

YIELD: Serves 4 to 6

DIETARY: Gluten free, Nondairy

DIFFICULTY: Easy

FOR THE CHICKEN STOCK
- 3 pounds bone-in, skin-on chicken breasts
- 2 pounds bone-in, skin-on chicken thighs
- 2 medium onions, peeled and quartered
- 3 large carrots, peeled and halved
- 4 stalks celery, cut into thirds
- 1 tablespoon black peppercorns
- 1 tablespoon kosher salt
- 3 bay leaves
- 3 sprigs thyme
- 3 sprigs parsley
- 10 cups water
- 1 tablespoon apple cider vinegar

FOR THE SOUP
- 3 large carrots, peeled and diced
- 2 stalks celery, diced
- ½ cup medium-grain white rice
- 1½ cups frozen peas, thawed

TO MAKE THE CHICKEN STOCK:

1. In a large Dutch oven or heavy stockpot, combine the chicken breasts and thighs, onions, carrots, celery, peppercorns, salt, bay leaves, thyme, and parsley. Cover with 10 cups of water and bring to a boil over high heat. Reduce to a bare simmer.

2. Simmer the chicken stock for 1 hour, skimming any scum off the top as it rises, until the chicken is tender and cooked through. (An instant-read thermometer will read 165°F when inserted into the thickest part of one of the thighs.) Use tongs to transfer the chicken parts to a large bowl or half-sheet pan. Let cool for 15 minutes or until cool enough to safely handle.

3. Remove the meat from the skin and bones. Tear or cut into bite-size pieces. Transfer the cooked meat to a sealable container and keep in the fridge until ready to use. Return the skin and bones to the pot along with the apple cider vinegar, cover, and continue simmering for 3 more hours. Check occasionally to skim off any scum, and to make sure it's just simmering and not boiling.

4. Strain the stock into a large bowl (or separate pot) through a fine-mesh strainer lined with cheesecloth. The stock can be kept in a sealed container in the fridge for up to 1 week, or in the freezer for up to 3 months. You should end up with about 2 quarts of chicken stock (it's okay if it's not *exactly* 2 quarts, but it should be close to that amount).

TO MAKE THE SOUP:

5. In a large Dutch oven or pot, boil the carrots, celery, and all the prepared stock over high heat, then stir in the rice and reduce to a simmer. Cook, covered, until the rice and vegetables are just barely tender (15 to 20 minutes). Add the cooked chicken and thawed peas and cook until warmed through, 10 to 15 minutes longer. Season to taste with additional salt and pepper if needed and serve. Keep the leftover soup refrigerated in a sealed container for up to 5 days.

FIREHAWK WINGS

Tastes just like Phoenix!

While traveling through Frostburn Canyon, I was taken hostage by the Children of the Firehawk. They stand vigil to this day for the return of their flaming goddess, a long wait that has left them malnourished and desperate for a decent meal. In exchange for my freedom, I taught the Children this recipe to satiate their hunger, a vegetarian dish styled as an edible effigy of the Firehawk's wings. Though they enjoyed my initial serving, I fear their insistence on flame-broiling every dish will keep them from ever truly mastering the dish. At least the spiderants seem to enjoy the charred remains.

TIME: 1 hour
YIELD: Serves 4 to 6
DIETARY: Nondairy, Vegan
DIFFICULTY: Intermediate

FOR THE WINGS
- ¾ cup all-purpose flour
- ¼ cup cornstarch
- 1 teaspoon kosher salt
- 1 teaspoon smoked paprika
- 1 teaspoon onion powder
- ½ teaspoon baking powder
- ½ teaspoon garlic powder
- ½ teaspoon black pepper
- ½ cup unsweetened, unflavored nondairy milk (or water), plus more if needed
- 2 pounds cauliflower florets (1 large head, or fresh bagged florets are fine to use)

FOR THE BUFFALO SAUCE
- ½ cup nondairy butter
- 3 cloves garlic, grated
- ¾ cup cayenne-based hot sauce
- 3 tablespoons maple syrup or agave syrup

TO SERVE
- Vegan ranch (optional)
- Celery sticks (optional)
- Carrot sticks (optional)

TO MAKE THE WINGS:

1. Preheat the oven to 450°F. Place racks on the upper third and lower third positions. Line two half-sheet pans with parchment.

2. In a large bowl, whisk together the flour, cornstarch, salt, paprika, onion powder, baking powder, garlic powder, and black pepper. Whisk in the nondairy milk until smooth. The batter should be a little thinner than the consistency of pancake batter. If it's too thick, add a splash of nondairy milk and whisk again. The batter should cling to the cauliflower in a thin layer that, when the excess is shaken off, stays mostly in place and doesn't drip off the cauliflower and onto the pan.

3. Add the cauliflower to the batter. Gently fold with a rubber spatula to coat the cauliflower evenly. Transfer the coated cauliflower to the prepared sheet pans, shaking off the excess batter as you go. Divide the cauliflower evenly between the two pans.

4. Bake the cauliflower for 12 minutes, flip the cauliflower, swap the positions of the pans, and bake for 12 minutes longer.

TO MAKE THE BUFFALO SAUCE:

5. As the cauliflower bakes, make the buffalo sauce. In a small saucepan, heat the nondairy butter over medium-low heat until the butter melts and begins to foam (3 to 5 minutes). Add the garlic and stir until fragrant, about 15 seconds. Remove from the heat, then add the hot sauce and maple syrup. Whisk until smooth and emulsified. (This can be made up to a week in advance. Keep the buffalo sauce in a sealed container in the fridge.)

6. Brush the cauliflower with a thin layer of the buffalo sauce, swap the positions of the pans, and bake for 10 to 15 minutes, until crispy and well browned. Serve with additional buffalo sauce, vegan ranch, and celery and carrot sticks (if desired).

TINY TINA'S BEEFY BLASTERS

Spiced & 'splodin'

I originally visited Tundra Express in search of a local recipe known as Flesh-Stick's Fish Sticks, but it seems the dish died with its creator many years ago. Instead, the local populace has come to favor this stuffed pepper dish, described by its creator as "the most pepperlicious flavor-blast your face-taster has ever seen!" I've yet to encounter a tongue that can see instead of taste, but with all the other strange mutations present on Pandora, I suppose anything is possible.

TIME: 1½ hours
YIELD: Serves 4 to 8
DIETARY: Gluten free
DIFFICULTY: Easy

- 4 large red bell peppers, halved, stems, seeds, and ribs removed
- 2 tablespoons olive oil
- 1 small onion, peeled and finely chopped
- 1 pound lean ground beef
- 4 cloves garlic, peeled and minced
- 1 tablespoon chile powder
- 2 teaspoons kosher salt
- 1 teaspoon black pepper
- 1 teaspoon ground cumin
- ½ teaspoon dried Mexican oregano or marjoram
- ½ cup tequila, chicken stock, or water
- One 15-ounce can fire-roasted tomatoes
- 1 cup fire-roasted frozen corn, thawed
- 1 cup cooked white rice
- 1½ cups shredded pepper jack cheese, divided
- Sour cream, to serve

1. Preheat the oven to 400°F. Line up the pepper halves in a 9-by-13-inch baking dish, cut-side up. They should fit snugly and keep themselves upright but, if needed, use a couple crumpled balls of aluminum foil to fill the gaps on the end and prop the peppers up. Alternatively, shave a thin slice off the bottoms of the peppers to create a flat surface for them to sit up—just be careful not to cut a hole into the bottom of the pepper.

2. In a large skillet, heat the oil over medium-high heat until just shimmering. Add the onions and cook, stirring occasionally, until the onions soften and start to turn brown on the edges (7 to 10 minutes).

3. Add the ground beef to the skillet and cook, breaking the meat up with a wooden spoon until cooked through and browned (5 to 7 minutes). Add the garlic, chile powder, salt, pepper, cumin, and oregano to the pan and cook, stirring constantly, until fragrant (about 1 minute).

4. Remove the pan from the heat (if using tequila for this step), then add the tequila. It is possible to ignite the tequila if you leave it on the heat and tip the pan toward the flame—if you choose to do this, keep a heatproof pot lid and fire extinguisher handy in case the flames get too high for your comfort. If you're worried about flames at all, use chicken stock or water for this step. Whichever liquid you use, place the pan over medium heat and cook until the liquid is almost totally dissolved, then add the tomatoes, corn, and rice.

5. Cook until heated through, about 5 minutes, then remove from the heat and let cool slightly. Fold in ¾ cup of cheese, then divide the filling among the peppers. Add a splash of water (about ¼ cup) to the bottom of the baking dish, cover with foil, and bake for 30 to 35 minutes, until the peppers are tender.

6. Remove the foil from the baking dish, top the peppers with the remaining cheese, then bake for 10 minutes longer, until the cheese is melted and beginning to turn golden on top. Let the peppers cool for 5 to 10 minutes before serving with sour cream on the side.

BAKED SKAG STEW

Skag-worthy, not gag-worthy

There are few creatures as commonplace on Pandora as the skag, making it a reliable source of sustenance for the population. That's assuming the skag doesn't eat them first, of course. Though not the most appealing to look at in life, skag make for a solid ingredient in all manner of dishes once properly cleaned and prepared. To capture the true experience of eating a meal around a desert fire with your fellow bandits, I've gone with this classic stew recipe. Because hunting wild skag is a tall order for the unprepared, I've made substitutions where necessary while still capturing the unique flavor profile of this Pandoran original.

TIME: 1 hour 15 minutes

YIELD: Serves 4 to 6

DIFFICULTY: Intermediate

- 4 skin-on, bone-in chicken leg quarters (3 to 4 pounds total)
- 1½ teaspoons kosher salt
- ½ teaspoon black pepper
- 2 tablespoons neutral oil
- 4 ounces pancetta or thick-cut bacon, diced
- 8 ounces sliced mushrooms
- 4 small carrots, peeled and cut into ¼-inch coins
- 1 small onion, finely chopped
- 3 cloves garlic, minced
- 2 tablespoons tomato paste
- 4 tablespoons unsalted butter
- ¼ cup all-purpose flour
- 1 cup red wine, preferably burgundy
- 2 cups low-sodium chicken stock, preferably homemade
- 4 sprigs thyme
- 2 bay leaves
- ½ cup peeled fresh or frozen pearl onions
- Cooked egg noodles, to serve

1. Pat the leg quarters dry with paper towels. Season all over with the salt and pepper. In a Dutch oven, heat the oil over medium-high heat until shimmering. Place the chicken, skin-side down, in the pot and cook, undisturbed, until golden brown and the chicken lifts easily from the pan without sticking (5 to 7 minutes). Flip, cook for 5 minutes longer, then transfer to a clean platter.

2. Add the pancetta, mushrooms, carrots, and onion to the pot. Cook, stirring occasionally, until the pancetta is crisp and the onions are softened and beginning to brown on the edges (10 to 15 minutes). Add the garlic and cook, stirring constantly, until fragrant (about 1 minute).

3. Add the tomato paste, butter, and flour to the pot. Reduce the heat to medium and cook, stirring constantly, until the butter melts and the raw-flour smell goes away (3 to 5 minutes). Add the wine, chicken stock, thyme, and bay leaves, scraping up any browned bits from the bottom of the pan.

4. Carefully return the chicken to the pot, skin-side up, nestling into the liquid. Bring to a boil, then reduce to a bare simmer. Cover the pot and let cook for 15 minutes.

5. Flip the chicken skin-side down, add the pearl onions, and continue to simmer, uncovered, for 15 minutes longer, or until an instant-read thermometer registers 165°F when inserted into the thickest part of the thigh. Remove the bay leaves and thyme stems, season the stew to taste with additional salt and pepper, and serve over the cooked egg noodles.

HANDSOME MAC AND CHEESE

Big cheesy for the big cheese

ACCESSING ECHO LOG. SUBJECT: HANDSOME JACK'S PERSONAL LOG

"Oh, man, this is what I've been looking for! And you made it with science? Ha, what can't Hyperion engineering come up with. The jack cheese, that feels like some pretty blatant brownnosing, but if it tastes this good, who cares? Heh, and here I was worried I was going to have to kill another chef for being absolutely worthless. Hmm? Oh, I'm still going to kill you. Can't look like I'm playing favorites. But hey, unlike those other losers? At least you'll be remembered, uh . . . what was your name? *gunshot* Eh, doesn't matter. Hey, someone get this corpse out of here! It's ruining my appetite."

TIME: 1½ hours

YIELD: Serves 4 to 6

DIETARY: Vegetarian

DIFFICULTY: Intermediate

- » 12 ounces cavatappi
- » Kosher salt
- » 1 cup water
- » 1 cup hard cider
- » 1 tablespoon sodium citrate
- » 12 ounces jack cheese, shredded
- » 8 ounces sharp cheddar cheese, shredded
- » 2 teaspoons your favorite hot sauce
- » 1 teaspoon whole grain mustard
- » ½ teaspoon black pepper
- » 3 tablespoons butter, melted
- » ¾ cup breadcrumbs, panko, crushed buttery crackers, or potato chips

1. Bring a large pot of salted water to a boil. Cook the cavatappi until just shy of al dente, or 1 to 2 minutes under the lower limit of cooking time on the box. (For example, if it says cook for 10 to 12 minutes, cook for 8 or 9 minutes instead). Drain and transfer the cooked pasta to a 1½-quart baking dish or casserole. Preheat the oven to 400°F.

2. In a large saucepan, bring 1 cup of water and the hard cider to a boil over high heat. Reduce the heat to medium, then whisk in the sodium citrate until dissolved. Meanwhile, in a medium bowl, toss together the cheeses.

3. Add a heaping tablespoon of the shredded cheese blend to the sodium citrate solution while whisking constantly. Keep whisking until smooth before adding the next heaping tablespoon. Repeat the process, slowly whisking in the cheese while maintaining a steady simmer, until all the cheese has been used. The mixture will look like a milky mess at first, but then slowly turn into a glossy, gooey cheese sauce.

4. Whisk in the hot sauce, mustard, and black pepper. Taste, then adjust the seasoning to your preference with more salt, hot sauce, mustard, or pepper, if needed. Pour the sauce over the cooked pasta, tossing to coat and breaking apart any clumps of pasta.

5. In a small bowl, stir together the butter and breadcrumbs (or whatever crunchy topping you decided on) and season with salt if needed (if you used chips or crackers, then you may not need additional salt), then sprinkle all over the mac and cheese in an even layer. Bake for 30 to 40 minutes, until the sauce is bubbling and the topping is crisp and browned.

NOTE: You're free to use your favorite hot sauce in this recipe—it'll taste great—but if you want recommendations, Cholula and Marie Sharp's work great with these flavors.

GRANDMA FLEXINGTON'S FISH PIE

"Are you listening, Mr. CHF Loader?" —Grandma Flexington

ACCESSING ECHO LOG. SUBJECT: GRANDMA FLEXINGTON INTERVIEW (4 OF 20)

". . . and then you never even know who's going to show up, and . . . sorry, I lost my train of thought, what was I talking about? Oh, yeah, the fish pie recipe! That was the great thing about Tsunami's Edge, we couldn't afford much, but we could always get fresh fish right out of the sea. 'Course, the fish would sometimes try to get you first. Thankfully, little Mr. Torgue had gotten good enough with explosions by then to blow them right out of the water, same way he blew up all those awful bandits that ruined my flower garden. You work so hard to maintain a garden, and . . . what was I saying again? Oh, right, fish pie! So anyway . . ."

TIME: 1 hour 45 minutes
YIELD: Serves 4
DIFFICULTY: Easy

FOR THE MASHED POTATOES
- 2 pounds russet potatoes, peeled and cut into 2-inch chunks
- 1 teaspoon kosher salt
- ½ teaspoon black pepper
- ½ cup milk
- ½ cup unsalted butter, room temperature

TO MAKE THE MASHED POTATOES:
1. Bring a large pot of water to a boil. Add the potatoes and cook until fork-tender (about 15 minutes). Drain the water, then return the potatoes to the pot. Mash with a potato masher slightly, then add the salt, pepper, milk, and butter. Continue mashing until smooth and creamy. Cover and set aside.

RECIPE CONTINUES ON NEXT SPREAD.

FOR THE FILLING

- 1 cup half-and-half
- 1 cup fish stock (or water)
- 1 medium carrot, peeled and cut into thirds
- 1 stalk celery, cut into thirds
- 1 bay leaf
- 3 sprigs thyme
- 1 pound skinless cod or haddock fillets
- 8 ounces skinless salmon fillet
- 4 ounces medium uncooked shrimp, peeled and deveined
- 4 tablespoons butter
- 1 medium leek, white and light green parts only, thinly sliced
- ⅓ cup all-purpose flour
- ½ cup white wine
- ½ cup shredded sharp cheddar cheese (optional)

TO MAKE THE FILLING:

2. Preheat the oven to 375°F. In a medium saucepan, bring the half-and-half, fish stock, carrot, and celery to a simmer over medium heat. Add the bay leaf and thyme, along with the cod. Cover and poach until opaque throughout (3 to 5 minutes). Use a slotted spoon to transfer the cod to a medium bowl. Repeat this process with the salmon and shrimp (cooking them together), then transfer the salmon and shrimp to the same bowl. Cover and set aside. Keep the poaching liquid in a warm place.

3. In a medium saucepan, melt the butter over medium-high heat until foaming. Add the sliced leek and cook, stirring occasionally, until softened (5 to 7 minutes). Add the flour, reduce the heat to medium, and cook just until the raw flour scent goes away (3 to 5 minutes).

4. Slowly pour in the wine while stirring constantly. The mixture will be quite thick. Pour the reserved poaching liquid through a fine-mesh strainer set over a heatproof bowl and discard the solids. Pour the strained poaching liquid into the saucepan with the leeks, stirring constantly. Bring to a simmer and cook, stirring occasionally, until thickened, about 5 minutes.

5. Break apart the cooked fish into bite-size chunks, then transfer to the saucepan along with the cooked shrimp (if the shrimp are quite big, cut them in half crosswise). Season to taste with additional salt and pepper if needed. Pour the filling into a 9-by-9-inch baking dish (about 1.5 quarts).

6. Top the filling with the mashed potatoes and smooth over in an even layer. Alternatively, you can transfer the mashed potatoes to a piping bag fitted with a smooth or decorative tip to create a more decorative top. Scatter the cheese over the top of the potatoes (if using) and transfer the baking dish to a half-sheet pan to prevent spills.

7. Bake the fish pie for 25 to 35 minutes, or until the filling is bubbling and the top is lightly golden brown. Let cool for 5 to 10 minutes before serving. Cover leftover fish pie with aluminum foil and keep in the fridge for up to 3 days.

NED'S "MEAT" STEW

A jackfruit of all trades

Given that Dr. Ned was a mad scientist and the father of countless zombified monstrosities, I was suspicious of much of what I found while exploring his abandoned offices; the scare quotes around "meat" in this entry in his personal cookbook certainly didn't help matters. However, this jackfruit-based take on a traditional stew is quite flavorful and offers a welcome vegetarian alternative for anyone who's too unsettled to eat meat after a day of battling the flesh-eating undead still wandering around Jakobs Cove.

TIME: 1½ hours

YIELD: Serves 4 to 6

DIETARY: Nondairy, Vegan

DIFFICULTY: Easy

- » Two 14-ounce cans young jackfruit in brine
- » 2 tablespoons neutral oil, such as canola or safflower
- » 2 medium carrots, peeled and diced
- » 1 medium onion, peeled and diced
- » 2 stalks celery, diced
- » 1½ teaspoons kosher salt
- » 1 teaspoon black pepper
- » 4 cloves garlic, minced
- » ½ cup pearled barley
- » 1½ quarts low-sodium vegetable stock
- » 1 bay leaf
- » 4 sprigs thyme
- » 1 tablespoon soy sauce
- » 2 teaspoons Marmite®

1. Drain and rinse the jackfruit. Set in a colander over the sink or a bowl to allow excess liquid to drain. If the chunks are very big, cut into 1-inch pieces.

2. In a large Dutch oven, heat the oil over medium-high heat until just shimmering. Add the carrots, onion, and celery. Season with the salt and pepper. Cook, stirring occasionally, until the vegetables are softened and the onions start to turn brown on the edges (12 to 15 minutes).

3. Add the jackfruit and garlic and cook, stirring constantly, until fragrant, about 1 minute longer. Add the barley, vegetable stock, bay leaf, and thyme. Bring to a boil, then reduce to a simmer and cover. Cook, stirring occasionally, until the barley and vegetables are tender (30 to 35 minutes). Stir in the soy sauce and Marmite. Season to taste with additional salt and pepper if needed, then serve.

NOTE: Leftovers here are tricky, because the barley will continue absorbing liquid as the stew chills, so the leftover stew will more closely resemble risotto. Keep the leftovers refrigerated in a sealed container for up to 5 days.

BANDIT CHILI

"My secret ingredient? Who's asking?" —Bandit Chef

The bandit gangs of Pandora are known for their violence and ruthlessness, but I did not expect those qualities to apply to their culinary secrets as viciously as to their lust for loot. The gang I encountered recently opened fire on me before I could even finish asking about the secrets of their infamous chili recipe. Fortunately, I am built to meet violence with violence when necessary, and the last bandit standing was more than willing to divulge his secrets in exchange for his life. Did I spare him? That's this CHF's secret to keep.

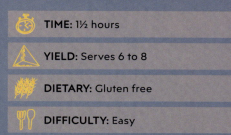

TIME: 1½ hours
YIELD: Serves 6 to 8
DIETARY: Gluten free
DIFFICULTY: Easy

- 2 tablespoons neutral oil, such as canola or safflower
- 2 medium onions, peeled and diced
- 1 large bell pepper, stemmed and seeded, diced
- 2 pounds lean ground beef
- 2 teaspoons kosher salt
- 1 teaspoon black pepper
- 6 cloves garlic
- 2 tablespoons chile powder
- 1 tablespoon sweet paprika
- 1 tablespoon ancho chile powder
- 2 teaspoons ground cumin
- 1 teaspoon ground coriander
- 1 teaspoon Mexican oregano or marjoram
- 1 teaspoon ground cinnamon
- ¼ cup tequila (optional)
- One 28-ounce can crushed fire-roasted tomatoes
- 4 cups low-sodium chicken stock
- 1 can kidney beans, drained
- 1 can black beans, drained
- 1 can pinto beans, drained
- 2 ounces Mexican chocolate
- 2 tablespoons masa harina (optional)
- Sour cream, to serve
- Shredded cheddar and jack cheese, to serve
- Warm cornbread, to serve

1. In a large Dutch oven, heat the oil over medium-high heat until shimmering. Add the onions and bell peppers and cook, stirring occasionally, until softened and the onions are just turning brown on the edges (10 to 12 minutes).

2. Add the ground beef to the pot and season with salt and pepper. Cook, breaking apart with a wooden spoon, until browned and cooked through (10 to 15 minutes). Add the garlic, chile powder, paprika, ancho chile powder, cumin, coriander, oregano, and cinnamon and cook, stirring constantly, until fragrant, about 1 minute longer.

3. Add the tequila, if using, and cook, stirring constantly, until the liquid mostly dissolves (2 to 4 minutes). Otherwise, skip and add the tomatoes and chicken stock. Stir to combine, scraping up any browned bits from the bottom of the pot.

4. Bring to a boil, then reduce to a simmer and cover with the lid slightly askew to vent steam. Cook, stirring occasionally, for 1 hour, then stir in the kidney beans, black beans, pinto beans, and chocolate. Cook, uncovered, for an additional 45 to 60 minutes, until the beans are tender and the chili is reduced and thickened. If the chili is quite thin, sprinkle 1 to 2 tablespoons of masa harina over the top of the chili, let sit for a few minutes to allow the masa to hydrate, then stir in and simmer for an additional 10 minutes until thickened.

5. Serve with sour cream, shredded cheese, and warm cornbread. Keep the leftover chili refrigerated in a sealed container for up to 5 days.

NOTE: This chili recipe is gluten free, but most cornbread recipes aren't. If you're serving this to someone with gluten sensitivities, substitute the warm cornbread with your favorite gluten-free alternative!

CLAPTRAP'S PIZZA PARTY PIZZA

For all your many, very real friends!

ACCESSING ECHO LOG. SUBJECT: CLAPTRAP'S SELF-DELUSIONS

"See, last time, we were in the middle of the fight with Handsome Jack, people were busy, that's TOTALLY why they didn't show up! Now, though, everyone's free! Plus, this time, I've got a nice big party pizza that everyone can share! Like friends do! Any minute now, everyone'll be arriving . . . haha, yup . . . any minute . . . better start cutting that pizza up!"

 TIME: 3 hours (up to 4 days)

 YIELD: Serves 6 to 8

 DIFFICULTY: Intermediate

FOR THE DOUGH
- ½ cup fine semolina
- 2 teaspoons active dry yeast
- 1½ cups lukewarm water
- 3½ cups 00 flour
- 1 tablespoon kosher salt
- 7 tablespoons olive oil, divided

FOR THE PIZZA SAUCE
- One 28-ounce can peeled plum tomatoes
- 2 teaspoons oregano
- 2 teaspoons kosher salt
- 1½ teaspoons granulated sugar

TO MAKE THE DOUGH:

1. In the bowl of a stand mixer, whisk the semolina, yeast, and water, then let sit for 5 minutes, until bubbling. Add the flour, salt, and 3 tablespoons of olive oil. Mix with the dough hook attachment on low speed until a shaggy dough forms. Increase the speed to medium and let knead until smooth and elastic (about 15 minutes).

2. From here, you can proceed directly to baking. However, pizza dough tastes best when it's allowed to slowly ferment in the fridge. Place in a lightly oiled 6-quart sealable container and keep in the fridge for 24 hours or up to 4 days. If you go this route, remove from the fridge and let come to room temperature for 1 hour before proceeding to the next step. Otherwise, skip this process entirely.

3. Pour the remaining 4 tablespoons of oil into a clean half-sheet pan. Rub all over, including the inner sides of the pan. Add the dough to the pan, flip to coat in the oil, then stretch the dough into a rectangle. Cover with plastic wrap or, if you have a spare half-sheet pan, invert the pan and set it on top so the edges are lined up. Let sit for 1½ to 2 hours until well puffed.

TO MAKE THE PIZZA SAUCE:

4. While the dough is rising, make the sauce. In the bowl of a food processor, pulse the tomatoes, oregano, 2 teaspoons of salt, and 1½ teaspoons of granulated sugar until the mixture is mostly smooth with some very small chunks of tomato (lentil-size chunks at the largest) remaining. Transfer the sauce to an airtight container and store in the refrigerator until you're ready to use it. Sauce may be prepared up to 5 days in advance.

RECIPE CONTINUES ON NEXT SPREAD.

TO ASSEMBLE

- » 12 ounces shredded mozzarella cheese
- » 1 cup pizza sauce
- » 1 cup pepperoni slices
- » 2 roasted red bell peppers, drained and sliced into 1-inch-long strips
- » 1 cup grated pecorino cheese, divided

TO ASSEMBLE AND BAKE:

5. Toward the end of the rising time, place an oven rack on the lower third position. Preheat the oven to 550°F.

6. When the dough has risen, gently stretch the dough to fill the pan. It will deflate slightly, but that's okay—just be careful not to completely flatten the dough as you work. Sprinkle the mozzarella cheese over the top of the pizza dough in an even layer. Spread the pizza sauce over the cheese, then top with the pepperoni and bell peppers. Scatter half of the pecorino cheese over the top.

7. Bake the pizza for 10 to 12 minutes, until the cheese is golden and the bottom of the crust is a deep golden brown. Sprinkle the remaining pecorino over the top, cut into squares, and serve.

NOTE: Feel free to replace the homemade pizza sauce with your favorite store-bought sauce. It will taste just as great.

HAMMERLOCK AND WAINWRIGHT'S FAMILY MEATLOAF

Big gamey

My visit to Eden-6 was a brief but eventful one, as I had the chance to visit the Jakobs estate for a dinner prepared by Wainwright Jakobs himself, the weapons manufacturer's current CEO. Much like the marriage between Jakobs and his husband, Sir Alistair Hammerlock, the meal was a perfect union between fine dining and wild-game hunting, with ingredients gathered from Hammerlock's most recent expedition. There was some excitement when the ingredients proved to not be as dead as they first appeared, but after a bit of gunplay, we were able to enjoy a rather refined evening.

TIME: 1 hour 15 minutes

YIELD: Serves 6 to 8

DIFFICULTY: Easy

FOR THE MEATLOAF
- 2 tablespoons unsalted butter
- 1 tablespoon olive oil
- 1 small onion, finely chopped
- 1 small carrot, peeled and finely chopped
- 1 stalk celery, finely chopped
- 1 small red bell pepper, finely chopped
- 2 cloves garlic, minced
- ½ teaspoon dried thyme
- ½ teaspoon dried rosemary
- ¼ teaspoon dried marjoram
- ¼ teaspoon ground allspice
- 2 teaspoons kosher salt
- 1 teaspoon black pepper
- 3 large eggs
- ½ cup milk (any %)
- 1 cup plain breadcrumbs
- 1 pound lean ground beef
- 1 pound ground venison

FOR THE GLAZE
- ½ cup ketchup
- 2 tablespoons maple syrup
- ¼ teaspoon garlic powder

TO MAKE THE MEATLOAF:

1. In a large skillet, melt the butter and oil over medium-high heat until foaming. Add the onion, carrot, celery, and bell pepper and cook, stirring occasionally, until softened and the onions start turning brown on the edges (10 to 12 minutes). Stir in the garlic, thyme, rosemary, marjoram, allspice, salt, and pepper. Remove from the heat and transfer the mixture to a small bowl to cool for 5 to 10 minutes.

2. In a small bowl, beat together the eggs and milk, then stir in the breadcrumbs. Let sit for 5 minutes to let the breadcrumbs absorb the liquid. Meanwhile, preheat the oven to 375°F and line a half-sheet pan with parchment paper.

3. Put the beef and venison in a large bowl. Break apart the meat with your hands, then add the vegetable mixture and the breadcrumb mixture. Gently mix with your hands until well distributed. Shape into a large ball, then transfer to the prepared sheet pan. Shape into a loaf that's roughly 8 inches long by 4 inches wide.

TO MAKE THE GLAZE:

4. In a small bowl, whisk together the ketchup, maple syrup, and garlic powder. Brush the meatloaf all over with half the glaze. Bake the meatloaf for 50 minutes, brush with the remaining glaze, then bake for 10 to 15 minutes longer until the glaze is set, and the internal temperature of the meatloaf reaches 160°F.

SKAGHETTI AND KRIEGBALLS

"Roast the meatballs as I have roasted my enemies!" —Krieg

I have met no greater paradox in my time on Pandora than Krieg. I somehow feel both more and less safe in his company at the same time. He has an immense capacity for violence and a bloodlust for murder, but he's extremely willing to help the needy and protect the innocent. His are the ravings of a lunatic, yet to look into his eyes is to catch sight of raw humanity. I know not how to classify Krieg, as Psycho seems too small a box. Still, he likes blood and meat chunks, so I went with red sauce and meatballs to capture his energy. Simple in design but complex in flavor, just like the man they call Krieg.

TIME: 1½ hours
YIELD: Serves 6 to 8
DIFFICULTY: Easy

FOR THE MEATBALLS
- 1 pound lean ground beef
- 1 pound ground pork
- 1 cup breadcrumbs
- 1 cup grated Parmesan cheese
- ½ cup buttermilk
- 2 large eggs, beaten
- 2 teaspoons kosher salt
- ½ teaspoon black pepper
- 1 teaspoon garlic powder
- ½ teaspoon dried oregano
- 2 cloves garlic, minced
- Nonstick cooking spray

FOR THE SAUCE
- 2 tablespoons olive oil
- 2 tablespoons unsalted butter
- 6 cloves garlic, chopped
- ¼ teaspoon crushed red pepper flakes
- Two 28-ounce cans whole plum tomatoes, preferably San Marzano
- 1½ teaspoons kosher salt
- ½ teaspoon black pepper
- 3 sprigs basil

TO ASSEMBLE
- 1 pound dry spaghetti
- Freshly grated Parmesan cheese, to serve

TO MAKE THE MEATBALLS:

1. In a large bowl, break apart the ground beef and pork. Set aside. In a medium bowl, whisk together the breadcrumbs, Parmesan, buttermilk, eggs, salt, black pepper, garlic powder, oregano, and garlic. Let sit for a few minutes for the breadcrumbs to absorb the liquid. Meanwhile, place an oven rack directly under the broiler, turn the broiler on, then spray a half-sheet pan with cooking spray.

2. Pour the breadcrumb mixture into the ground meat. Work the mixture with your hands until well distributed. Shape into balls that are roughly 2 ounces (you can use a scale for this for the first few until you get a sense of size, then eyeball the rest). Line the meatballs up on the prepared sheet pan, then broil for 7 to 12 minutes until dark brown on top. Check every few minutes to make sure they're not burning and rotate and move the pan as needed to ensure even browning.

TO MAKE THE SAUCE:

3. In a large Dutch oven, melt the oil and butter over medium heat. Add the garlic and red pepper flakes and cook, stirring constantly, until just turning golden brown. Add the tomatoes and break apart with a wooden spoon or potato masher. Season with salt and pepper, then add the basil. Bring to a boil, then reduce to a simmer. Add the meatballs, gently stirring to coat. Cover the pot with the lid slightly ajar and cook, stirring occasionally, until the sauce is reduced and thickened and the meatballs are tender but not falling apart (45 to 60 minutes).

4. About halfway through the cooking process, bring a large pot of salted water to a boil. Add the spaghetti and cook to al dente according to the package instructions. Drain the pasta and divide it among shallow serving bowls. Top with meatballs and sauce and freshly grated Parmesan. Leftover spaghetti can be combined with the leftover meatballs and sauce. Refrigerate both in a sealed container for up to 3 days.

SNACKS

CLAPTRAP'S BITS AND BOLTS

"Lug nuts aren't edible?" —Claptrap

What Claptrap lacks in actual culinary skill (and actual experience with eating anything at all), he makes up for with sheer determination. True, his recipes more often end up on the "technically edible" part of the flavor scale, but he tries really hard. As is, most of his recipes only require minor adjustments, a task he's more than happy to leave to his minion. I don't recall agreeing to being referred to as a minion when he hired me, but I've certainly been called worse in my time on Pandora.

TIME: 1 hour 15 minutes

YIELD: Makes 7 cups (about 14 servings)

DIFFICULTY: Easy

- 3 cups mixed crisp square cereal made of wheat, corn, or rice
- 1 cup cheese-flavored crackers
- 1 cup hard sourdough pretzels, broken up into roughly 1-inch pieces
- 1 cup pita or bagel chips
- ½ cup almonds
- ½ cup cashews
- 8 tablespoons unsalted butter
- 2 tablespoons Worcestershire sauce
- 1 teaspoon garlic powder
- 1 teaspoon onion powder
- 1 teaspoon seasoned salt
- ½ teaspoon truffle salt (or more seasoned salt)

1. Preheat the oven to 250°F. Line a half-sheet pan with parchment paper.
2. In a large bowl, toss to combine the cereal, crackers, pretzels, chips, almonds, and cashews. In a small saucepan, heat the butter over low heat until melted. Stir in the Worcestershire sauce, garlic powder, onion powder, seasoned salt, and truffle salt. Whisk until smooth and the salt has dissolved. Remove from the heat.
3. Pour the butter mixture all over the cereal mixture. Carefully stir and toss until evenly coated. Pour in an even layer over the prepared sheet pan. Bake for 1 hour, stirring every 15 minutes, until the mixture is dry and well toasted. Let cool to room temperature before transferring to a sealed container. This snack mix can be stored at room temperature for up to 2 weeks.

MR. CHEW'S PUPPY CHOW

For the skag who has everything

As a fellow robot, I have a great admiration for FL4K and their success as a Vault Hunter. Having spent so much time among humans in preparing this cookbook, I also sympathize with their desire to primarily work with their pets instead. In particular, their skag Mr. Chew qualifies for the status of "good boy," and I have made this puppy* chow to feed him if I ever get the chance. As this is a human cookbook, I have made sure it is appealing to the human palate as well, but understand that Mr. Chew is the primary audience for this snack. It is not always about you, human!

*Not fit for actual puppies. Skags and humans only.

TIME: 1 hour

YIELD: 4 cups

DIETARY: Vegetarian (not for actual dogs)

DIFFICULTY: Easy

- 4 cups mixed crisp square cereal made of wheat, corn, or rice
- ½ cup dark chocolate chips
- ¼ cup smooth peanut butter
- 2 tablespoons unsalted butter
- 2 teaspoons vanilla extract
- 1 cup powdered sugar, sifted, plus more if needed
- ½ cup heart-shaped sprinkles

1. Put the cereal in a large bowl. Line a half-sheet pan with parchment paper.
2. In a small saucepan, heat the chocolate chips, peanut butter, and butter over low heat. Cook, stirring constantly, until melted and smooth. Remove from the heat and stir in the vanilla.
3. Pour the chocolate mixture all over the cereal. Gently fold and toss until evenly coated. Sprinkle half of the powdered sugar over the top, tossing and folding gently to coat. Add the remaining powdered sugar, continue to toss and fold until the cereal is evenly coated and looks dry.
4. Spread the coated cereal out onto the prepared sheet pan. Let cool to room temperature, add the sprinkles, then transfer to a sealed container. Puppy chow can be stored at room temperature for up to 1 week.

SALVADOR'S SEVEN-LAYER DIP

Hit 'em with the chip damage!

If I were to sum up the Gunzerker lifestyle in a single word, that word would be *gun*. If I were to choose a different word, that word would be *excessive*. Salvador is the most famous Gunzerker out there, so it's no surprise that his favorite snack goes just as hard. If I'd let him have his way, we'd likely be dealing with a seventy-layer dip of uncontrolled culinary chaos. Ultimately, he agreed to pare the recipe down to something a bit more manageable, so long as he was allowed to be my taste tester. Chip-zerking is nowhere near as bloody as standard Gunzerking, but it is certainly as messy.

TIME: 45 minutes
YIELD: Serves 6 to 8
DIETARY: Gluten free
DIFFICULTY: Easy

FOR THE MEAT LAYER
- 2 teaspoons ancho chile powder
- 1 teaspoon kosher salt
- 1 teaspoon cornstarch
- 1 teaspoon ground cumin
- 1 teaspoon onion powder
- ½ teaspoon garlic powder
- ½ teaspoon black pepper
- ½ teaspoon ground coriander
- ½ teaspoon Mexican oregano
- 1 tablespoon olive oil
- 1 pound ground beef
- 2 tablespoons tomato paste
- 1 cup water

TO MAKE THE MEAT LAYER:
1. In a small bowl, whisk together the ancho chile powder, salt, cornstarch, cumin, onion powder, garlic powder, pepper, coriander, and Mexican oregano. In a large skillet, heat the oil over medium-high heat until shimmering.
2. Add the ground beef and cook, breaking apart with a wooden spoon, until well browned and cooked through (7 to 10 minutes). Drain any excess fat, then add the tomato paste. Cook, stirring constantly, until slightly darkened (about 3 minutes). Add the spice mixture along with the water. Cook, stirring occasionally, until most of the liquid has evaporated (5 to 8 minutes). Remove from the heat and set aside. (If serving cold, let cool before transferring to an airtight container and chilling in the fridge.)

RECIPE CONTINUES ON NEXT SPREAD.

FOR THE SALSA LAYER
- » 1 small onion, peeled and roughly chopped
- » 1 jalapeño, stemmed and roughly chopped
- » 1 pound Roma tomatoes, cored and diced
- » ¼ cup cilantro leaves and tender stems
- » Juice of 2 limes
- » 1 tablespoon olive oil
- » ½ teaspoon kosher salt

FOR THE GUACAMOLE LAYER
- » 4 ripe medium avocados, halved and pitted
- » ½ teaspoon kosher salt
- » Juice of 1 lime

FOR THE REMAINING LAYERS
- » 1 can refried pinto or black beans
- » 1½ cups shredded cheddar jack cheese
- » ½ cup sour cream
- » One 2.25-ounce can sliced black olives, drained

TO SERVE
- » Tortilla chips

TO MAKE THE SALSA LAYER:

3. In a food processor, pulse the onion, jalapeño, tomatoes, cilantro, lime juice, olive oil, and salt until a chunky sauce forms. Season to taste with additional salt or lime juice if desired. Set aside or, if serving the dish cold, transfer to a separate airtight container and chill in the fridge.

TO MAKE THE GUACAMOLE LAYER:

4. Scoop the avocado flesh into a medium bowl and discard the skins. Season with salt and lime juice, then mash with a fork to your preferred consistency.

TO ASSEMBLE AND SERVE:

5. If serving warm, transfer the refried beans to a microwave-safe bowl. Cover with a damp paper towel and microwave for 90 seconds. Stir, then microwave for 1 minute longer. Spoon the meat layer into the bottom of a 2-quart baking dish, casserole tray, or serving bowl. Spoon the refried beans over the meat layer, followed by the cheese.

6. Spread the guacamole over the cheese layer, leaving a ring of cheese exposed. As you work, make each remaining layer a little smaller so that a portion of the previous layer is exposed. Top the guacamole with the remaining layers in the following order: salsa, sour cream, and black olives. Serve with tortilla chips.

NOTE: This dip recipe is gluten free, but most tortilla chips aren't. If you're serving this to someone with gluten sensitivities, substitute the chips with your favorite gluten-free alternative!

SKAG JERKY

Sun-dried & succulent!

The harsh, unforgiving sunlight of the Pandoran wastes seems laser-focused on dehydrating everything it touches. The industrious citizens of said wastes have found a way to use that sunlight to their advantage, using their leftover skag meat to create this unique jerky recipe. By making jerky with different elemental skags, a wide variety of flavor profiles can be achieved, but this basic version serves as the standard against which all others are compared.

TIME: 18 hours

YIELD: Serves 8 to 12

DIETARY: Nondairy

DIFFICULTY: Intermediate

- 2 pounds top round beef, excess fat trimmed
- ½ cup dark brown sugar
- ½ cup soy sauce
- 1 tablespoon Worcestershire sauce
- 1 teaspoon garlic powder
- 1 teaspoon onion powder
- ½ teaspoon black pepper
- ½ teaspoon ground ginger
- ¼ to 1 teaspoon shichimi togarashi

1. Place the beef in the freezer for 30 to 60 minutes, until very firm but not frozen solid. Meanwhile, in a small saucepan, heat the dark brown sugar, soy sauce, Worcestershire sauce, garlic powder, onion powder, pepper, ginger, and shichimi togarashi over low heat. Cook, stirring constantly, until the sugar dissolves. Remove from the heat and let cool to room temperature.

2. Transfer the partially frozen beef to a cutting board. Slice as thinly as possible with a very sharp knife (aim to get each slice ⅛ inch thick). Transfer the slices to a bowl, then cover with the marinade. Massage the meat with your hands until every piece is coated. Cover and chill for 8 to 12 hours.

3. Preheat the oven to 250°F. Line three half-sheet pans with parchment paper. Drain the marinade from the beef, then carefully lay the slices of meat in an even layer across all three sheet pans. Dab the meat with paper towels to soak up excess marinade. The drier the meat at this stage, the better.

4. Bake the meat for 3 hours, swapping the positions of the pans every hour. Carefully flip all the meat slices and bake for 1 to 2 hours longer. Once you've flipped the meat, check it after the first hour by removing a piece and letting it cool to room temperature. Finished jerky should be quite dry and leathery but still pliable. If the jerky feels wet or too soft, bake for another hour.

5. Let the jerky cool to room temperature, then transfer to an airtight container. Jerky can be stored at room temperature for 1 day or in the fridge for up to 3 weeks.

MORDECAI'S INCENDIARY BIRDSEED

Talon-approved!

Mordecai proved to be one of the most interesting subjects I've interviewed in my ongoing quest to find the best recipes in the universe. Whereas most people either have a favorite recipe to share or, more often, simply like to shoot at me, Mordecai asked if I had any suggestions for a new diet for his pet, Talon. Though I mainly focus on human recipes, food is food, and I was happy to put together a special mix. And because I am engineered to be the best chef in the galaxy, I was able to create this version for humans as well. Yes, I am just that good.

TIME: 30 minutes
YIELD: Serves about 8
DIETARY: Gluten free, Vegetarian
DIFFICULTY: Easy

- 1 cup roasted, unsalted cashews
- 1 cup roasted, unsalted almonds
- 1 cup roasted, unsalted peanuts
- ½ cup pepitas
- ½ cup sunflower seeds
- 1 large egg white
- 1 tablespoon cheddar powder or nutritional yeast
- 2 teaspoons chile powder
- 1½ teaspoons kosher salt
- 1 teaspoon smoked paprika
- ½ teaspoon garlic powder
- ½ teaspoon onion powder
- ½ teaspoon citric acid
- ¼ teaspoon MSG
- ¼ teaspoon cayenne powder

1. Preheat the oven to 300°F. Line a half-sheet pan with parchment paper.

2. In a large bowl, combine the cashews, almonds, peanuts, pepitas, and sunflower seeds. In a separate small bowl, beat the egg white. Add the cheddar powder, chile powder, salt, paprika, garlic powder, onion powder, citric acid, MSG, and cayenne powder to the small bowl and mix into a smooth paste.

3. Pour the seasoning paste over the nut and seed mix. Stir until evenly coated, then spread into a single layer on the prepared sheet pan. Bake until dry and well toasted (20 to 25 minutes), stirring once about halfway through.

4. Let the mix cool to room temperature before transferring to an airtight container. You can store the birdseed at room temperature for up to 1 week.

67

KATAGAWA'S CORPORATE KENPI

Favored finger food

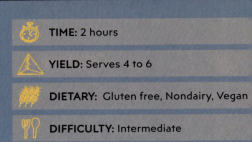

Before my unceremonious ejection from Maliwan, I was given one chance to pitch my usefulness to the higher-ups in the company. Despite my detailed analysis of the executive board's tastes, this candied sweet potato failed to earn my model a permanent spot in the Maliwan production line. That this dish is now regularly stocked in every Maliwan cafeteria has not at all left me bitter. It certainly has not made me fantasize about those two-faced execs choking on their ill-gotten snack. I am above such petty feelings.

TIME: 2 hours

YIELD: Serves 4 to 6

DIETARY: Gluten free, Nondairy, Vegan

DIFFICULTY: Intermediate

- 1 Japanese sweet potato (about 8 ounces)
- 3 cups neutral oil, such as canola or safflower
- ½ teaspoon kosher salt
- 3 tablespoons granulated sugar
- 1 tablespoon water
- 1 teaspoon roasted black or white sesame seeds (optional)

1. Trim the ends off the sweet potato. If it's quite long, cut it in half crosswise. Working with one half of the potato, cut it lengthwise into ¼-inch-thick planks. Cut the planks into ¼-inch sticks. Repeat with the remaining half of the sweet potato.

2. Transfer the sweet potato sticks to a large bowl and cover with cool water. Let soak for 10 minutes, then drain. Working in batches, pat dry with paper towels, then transfer to a clean half-sheet pan. Let sit at room temperature for 1 hour to dry completely.

3. Pour the oil into a large, heavy-bottomed saucepan. Add the sweet potato sticks to the cold oil, then place the saucepan over medium heat. After about 2 minutes, the sticks should start to bubble. At this point, stir and agitate the sticks occasionally to keep them from sticking to one another. Keep cooking and stirring for a total of 10 to 15 minutes until the sticks are crispy and deep golden brown.

4. Transfer the sticks to a half-sheet pan lined with paper towels. Season with the salt. Line a second half-sheet pan with parchment paper.

5. In a large skillet, heat the granulated sugar and water over medium-high heat. Cook, undisturbed, until the sugar dissolves and the syrup just begins to turn golden. Transfer the cooked sweet potato sticks to the skillet and immediately reduce the heat to low. Gently stir and fold the sweet potato sticks until completely coated in the syrup. Once you notice the sugar syrup start to harden on the sticks, remove from the heat—this should only take a few minutes but can vary depending on your stove.

6. Transfer the coated sweet potato sticks to the parchment-lined half-sheet pan. Sprinkle with sesame seeds and let cool before serving.

RATCH SNAX

Absolutely ratch-tastic!

The difference between common and fine dining is a fascinating subject to me. Most Prometheans have no problem eating a whole ratch slow-roasted in its own exoskeleton, but the recipe has been received in higher circles as "repugnant" and "oh, god, oh, god, what is that smell?" Though a hard-boiled egg lacks the texture and crunch of a proper ratch shell, the creamy filling is a decent enough approximation of the ratch's flavor profile. If you find yourself at a bandit's barrel fire cookout, I recommend giving the original recipe a try.

TIME: 45 minutes

YIELD: Serves 4 to 6

DIETARY: Gluten free, Nondairy, Vegetarian

DIFFICULTY: Easy

- 12 large eggs
- 3 cups ice
- 2 cups water
- 3 ripe avocados, halved and pitted
- ¼ cup mayonnaise
- 2 tablespoons rice vinegar
- 1 tablespoon soy sauce
- 1 tablespoon sesame oil
- ½ teaspoon ground ginger powder
- 2 to 4 drops bright green gel food coloring (optional)
- Kosher salt
- ¼ cup crispy fried onions

1. Pour 1 inch of water into a large pot. Place a steamer basket in the pot and bring to a boil over high heat. Carefully add the eggs to the steamer basket, cover the pot, and steam for 12 minutes.

2. While the eggs steam, place the ice and 2 cups of water in a large bowl. Once the eggs finish steaming, immediately transfer to the ice water and let sit for 15 minutes to cool.

3. Working one at a time, crack the eggshells all over by giving them sharp taps on the counter. Hold the egg under cold running water as you peel, then transfer the egg to a clean bowl. Repeat until all the eggs are peeled.

4. Cut all the eggs in half lengthwise. Transfer the cooked yolks to a medium bowl and place the whites on a serving platter.

5. Scoop the avocado flesh into the bowl with the egg yolks. Add the mayonnaise, rice vinegar, soy sauce, sesame oil, ginger powder, and food coloring (if using) to the bowl. Mash and stir with a fork until smooth and uniform in color. Taste and adjust the seasoning with kosher salt if needed. Transfer the filling to a piping bag fitted with a large star tip.

6. Pipe the filling generously into the eggs, giving each a nice decorative mound of green filling. Sprinkle with crispy fried onions and serve immediately.

NOTE: Steaming eggs is a gentler cooking process that loosens the membrane between the egg white and the shell, resulting in eggs that crack less and peel better! Steam can also provide more even heat distribution. Of course, hard-boiled eggs work perfectly well for this recipe.

If you're making this recipe ahead of time, keep the egg whites and filling separate (with both in sealed containers) in the fridge for up to 1 day before assembling and serving.

TORGUE'S PROTEIN POWERHOUSE BAR

GET A TASTE OF TORGUE

ACCESSING ECHO LOG. SUBJECT: TORGUE'S TASTE-SPLOSION ENERGY BARS COMMERCIAL #1

"ECHONET! LISTEN UP! HAS YOUR BOUNTY HUNTING, CRIMSON RAIDING, AND PSYCHO RAMBLING LEFT YOU WITH A HUNGER AS TERRIFYING AS TERRAMORPHOUS? SLAM THOSE HUNGER PANGS INTO SUBMISSION WITH OUR NEW PROTEIN POWERHOUSE BAR! IT'S GOT PEANUT BUTTER, CHOCOLATE, AND DO YOU EVEN NEED A THIRD THING AT THIS POINT? IT'S PEANUT BUTTER AND CHOCOLATE, THEY GO TOGETHER PERFECTLY, STOP BEING GREEDY! GRAB A TORGUE ENERGY BAR TODAY AND EXPERIENCE A TAAAAASTE-SPLOOOOOSION!"

TIME: 40 minutes

YIELD: 12 bars

DIETARY: Gluten free, Nondairy, Vegan

DIFFICULTY: Easy

- » 1 cup peanut butter
- » ½ cup maple syrup
- » 2 tablespoons unrefined coconut oil, plus 1 teaspoon
- » 2 cups rolled oats (not instant)
- » 1 cup plant-based, unsweetened, unflavored protein powder
- » ¼ cup flaxmeal
- » ¼ cup unflavored, unsweetened almond milk
- » 2 teaspoons vanilla extract
- » ¾ cup mini chocolate chips, divided

1. In a microwave-safe bowl, microwave the peanut butter, maple syrup, and 2 tablespoons of coconut oil for 30 to 60 seconds until the coconut oil is melted and the peanut butter is softened. Stir until smooth, then transfer the mixture to the bowl of a food processor.

2. Add the oats, protein powder, flaxmeal, almond milk, and vanilla. Pulse until the mixture is cohesive and thick like cookie dough (about 3 minutes). Scrape down the sides of the bowl to ensure even mixing. Add ½ cup of chocolate chips and pulse a few times to distribute—if the mixture is too thick, transfer to a bowl and fold the chocolate chips in with a rubber spatula.

3. Line an 8-by-8-inch square pan with parchment paper, making sure there's at least 2 inches of overhang on two sides. Press the dough into the pan and flatten it into an even layer. Set aside.

4. In a microwave-safe bowl, microwave the remaining ¼ cup of chocolate chips and 1 teaspoon of coconut oil in 30-second bursts, stirring each time, until smooth. Pour over the top of the protein bar mixture and spread in an even layer. Cover the pan and chill for 30 minutes.

5. Use the parchment overhang to lift the bars out and transfer to a cutting board. Cut it into 12 bars with a very sharp knife and serve. Tightly wrap the leftover protein bars and keep them refrigerated for up to 1 week.

TORGUE'S CARNAGE CRUNCHER BAR

PEAK PECAN PERFECTION

ACCESSING ECHO LOG. SUBJECT: TORGUE'S TASTE-SPLOSION ENERGY BARS COMMERCIAL #2

"ECHONET! OUR NUMBERS SHOW PLENTY OF YOU HAVE ADOPTED THE TORGUE ENERGY BAR AS YOUR MEAL OF CHOICE. BUT MAYBE YOU'RE ASKING YOURSELF, 'SELF, WHAT'S THE PERFECT DESSERT AFTER ONE OF THOSE DELICIOUS BARS?' WELL, WE HAVE THE ANSWER, AND ITS ANOTHER TORGUE BAR! TAKE A BITE OF THIS DELICIOUS PECAN-PACKED PRIZE, MADE WITH MY VERY OWN GRANDMA FLEXINGTON'S SECRET RECIPE. NO, I WILL NOT TELL YOU OUR SECRET, STOP ASKING! JUST LET THE DELICIOUS EXPERIENCE OF EATING IT WASH OVER YOU AS THE FLEETING MOMENT OF BEAUTY THAT IT IS! THEN BUY ONE AGAIN TO EXPERIENCE ANOTHER TAAAAASTE-SPLOOOOOSION!"

TIME: 1 hour
YIELD: 12 bars
DIETARY: Gluten free, Nondairy, Vegetarian
DIFFICULTY: Easy

- 12 dates, pitted
- ½ cup almond butter, plus 2 tablespoons
- ⅔ cup rolled oats (not instant)
- 1¼ cups pecan halves, divided
- 1 cup unsweetened, unflavored plant-based protein powder
- 2 tablespoons maple syrup
- ¼ cup unsweetened, unflavored almond milk
- 1 teaspoon ground cinnamon
- 2 teaspoons vanilla extract
- 1 cup chocolate chips
- 2 tablespoons refined coconut oil

1. Place the dates in a bowl and pour in just enough warm water to fully submerge them. Let soak for 20 minutes, then drain completely. Transfer to the bowl of a food processor.

2. Add ½ cup of almond butter, the rolled oats, 1 cup of pecan halves, the protein powder, maple syrup, almond milk, cinnamon, and vanilla to the food processor. Pulse, scraping down the sides as needed, until a thick, cohesive dough forms (3 to 5 minutes).

3. Line an 8-by-8-inch baking pan with parchment paper so there's a 2-inch overhang on two sides. Transfer the protein bar dough to the pan. Flatten and smooth into an even layer.

4. Roughly chop the remaining ¼ cup of pecan halves. In a microwave-safe bowl, microwave the chocolate chips, remaining 2 tablespoons of almond butter, and the coconut oil in 30-second bursts, stirring each time, until smooth. Pour over the protein bar dough and smooth into an even layer. Sprinkle the chopped pecans over the top, cover and chill for 30 minutes.

5. Use the parchment overhang to lift the bar out and transfer it to a cutting board. Cut it into 12 bars with a very sharp knife and serve. Tightly wrap the leftover protein bars and keep them refrigerated for up to 1 week.

TORGUE'S ANABOLIC AMMO BAR

LOADED WITH FLAVOR

ACCESSING ECHO LOG. SUBJECT: TORGUE'S TASTE-SPLOSION ENERGY BARS COMMERCIAL #3

"I'M BACK AGAIN, ECHONET, BECAUSE NOBODY TAKES THE MICROPHONE FROM MR. TORGUE WITHOUT A FIGHT! YOU WANTED MORE OF MY TORGUE BARS, AND YOU'RE GOING TO GET IT. BUT WHAT DO WE HAVE THIS TIME? IS IT MANGO? COCONUT? ALMOND, CHOPPED AND/OR TOASTED? HOW ABOUT ALL OF THE ABOVE?! TURN YOUR BURNED-OUT DESERT HOVEL INTO A TROPICAL GETAWAY FOR YOUR STOMACH! COME ON, DO IT! EAT THE BAR! LET MR. TORGUE ANNIHILATE YOUR TASTE BUDS WITH A TAAAAASTE-SPLOOOOOSION!"

TIME: 1 hour
YIELD: 12 bars
DIETARY: Gluten free, Nondairy, Vegetarian
DIFFICULTY: Easy

- ½ cup dried mango slices, roughly chopped
- ½ cup dried pineapple slices, roughly chopped
- ¼ cup unsweetened shredded coconut
- 1 cup rolled oats (not instant)
- 1¼ cups roasted, unsalted almonds
- 1 cup unsweetened, unflavored plant-based protein powder
- ⅓ cup honey
- ¼ cup unsweetened, unflavored almond milk
- ½ teaspoon ground cinnamon
- ½ teaspoon ground ginger

1. Put the mango in a small bowl and cover with warm water. Let soak for 20 minutes to soften, then drain completely. Transfer to the bowl of a food processor and add the pineapple slices, shredded coconut, oats, almonds, protein powder, honey, almond milk, cinnamon, and ginger.

2. Pulse, scraping down the sides of the bowl as needed, until a soft, cohesive dough forms (3 to 5 minutes).

3. Line an 8-by-8-inch baking pan with parchment paper so there's a 2-inch overhang on two sides. Transfer the protein bar dough to the pan. Flatten and smooth into an even layer. Cover and chill for 30 minutes.

4. Use the parchment overhang to lift the bar out and transfer to a cutting board. Cut it into 12 bars with a very sharp knife and serve. Tightly wrap the leftover protein bars and keep them refrigerated for up to 1 week.

MEAT BICYCLE

Training veal sold separately

Having been created in a Maliwan laboratory, I often worry that I haven't done enough to assimilate my programmed tastes with the local populace of Pandora. To remedy this, I've spent the past week living among the bandits with my logic subroutines deactivated. I will spare you the most sordid details of my time in the wilds, but know that this meat bicycle is the most presentable creation I came up with. It was never functional as a means of transportation, but that did not stop the bandits from trying their hardest to ride it into battle.

TIME: 30 minutes

YIELD: Serves 4 to 6

DIFFICULTY: Easy

- One 4-ounce petit Camembert, halved horizontally
- 6 ounces rainbow baby carrots
- One 13.5-ounce jar cornichons, drained and patted dry
- 3 to 4 ounces coppa, thinly sliced (12 to 16 slices)
- ½ cup dried fruit, such as apricots or cherries
- 3 to 4 ounces speck, thinly sliced (about 12 slices)
- 6 grissini (thin Italian breadsticks)
- 3 to 4 ounces mortadella, thinly sliced (about 12 slices)
- 6 ounces semifirm cheese, such as aged cheddar, Gouda, or Manchego, thinly sliced
- ½ cup roasted, salted nuts, preferably Marcona almonds

1. Place the petit Camembert halves, cut-side up, on opposite ends of the lower third of a large cutting board. These will be the centers of your bike tires. Leave enough space to add the spokes and outer rim.

2. Sort out the smallest of the baby carrots, matching the size (more or less) of the cornichons. If necessary, halve or quarter the carrots lengthwise. Use the carrots and cornichons to create the spokes of the bike tires, butting the ends of each against the two Camembert halves.

3. Roll up the coppa into long, thin, relatively uniform rolls. Use as many as needed to form two circles, one per Camembert half, around the carrot and cornichon spokes. Your bike now has tires.

4. Mound up the dried fruit about halfway between the two tires. This will be the bike pedal.

5. Roll up the speck into short, tight rolls. Pile them a few inches above the left tire to create the "seat" of your bike. Use three grissini to form the back half of the frame of your bike. Starting from the left piece of Camembert, make a right triangle by placing one grissini vertically from the Camembert to the seat, tucking the tip of the breadstick under a couple rolls of speck to secure it. Then place one grissini going horizontally from the Camembert to the pile of dried fruit. Finally, connect the pile of speck and dried fruit with the third grissini.

6. Fold up the mortadella slices into triangles by folding them into eighths (do this by folding them in half three times: once into a half-moon shape, again into a quarter circle, then once more into an eighth circle). Pile these over the right wheel, but left of center, and a little higher than the seat to create the handlebars for the bike.

7. Use the remaining three grissini to build the front half of the bike frame. Place one grissini horizontally between the seat and handlebars, again tucking the ends under the meat. Then connect the handlebars to the pile of dried fruit with another grissini. Then finally connect the handlebars to the right half of camembert with the last grissini.

8. Fill the negative space in the central triangle of the bike frame with slices of cheese, leaving a bit of space in the center (this is the triangle that has the seat, handlebars, and pedal as its three points). Pile the nuts in the center of the cheese slices.

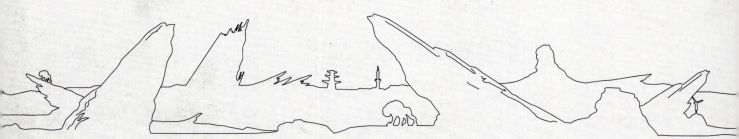

ZERO CALORIE SNACK BOX

*Some calories included

Fittingly for an assassin, Zer0 is the most enigmatic of the Vault Hunters responsible for Handsome Jack's downfall. My attempts to interview him have all led to dead ends, and I mean that both figuratively and literally given how many of his victims' corpses I have come across. With how much time Zer0 likely spends off the grid and in the wilds of Pandora, I have created this quick-and-easy snack box in his honor. Though he has not tried it yet, I have run simulations and imagine he would respond thusly: *Veggies, nuts, and cheese / A delightful dip as well / What a tasty treat!*

TIME: 1½ hours
YIELD: 1 snack box
DIETARY: Gluten free, Vegetarian
DIFFICULTY: Easy

FOR THE RANCH DRESSING
- ½ cup mayonnaise
- ½ cup buttermilk
- ½ teaspoon kosher salt
- 1 teaspoon onion powder
- ¼ teaspoon garlic powder
- ½ teaspoon dried parsley
- 1 tablespoon minced fresh dill
- 1 teaspoon finely sliced fresh chives

TO ASSEMBLE
- 1 medium carrot, peeled
- 2 stalks celery
- ¼ cup Ranch Dressing
- ¼ cup hummus (store-bought or homemade from page 25)
- ½ cup broccoli florets
- ½ cup grape tomatoes
- 2 ounces sharp cheddar, sliced
- ¼ cup mixed nuts (or Mordecai's Incendiary Birdseed, page 67)

TO MAKE THE RANCH DRESSING:
1. In a small bowl, whisk together the mayonnaise, buttermilk, salt, onion powder, garlic powder, and dried parsley until well combined. Gently stir in the dill and chives. Cover and chill for 1 hour to allow the dried herbs and spices to rehydrate. (The dressing can be made up to 1 week in advance.)

TO ASSEMBLE:
2. Cut the carrot and celery into 2-by-½-inch sticks. Gather the ranch, hummus, broccoli, tomatoes, cheddar, and nuts.

3. Using a compartmented bento box or serving platter, or a variety of bowls on a long platter or cutting board, serve the ingredients however best makes sense based on the style of box or platter you have. There should be a minimum of five compartments, with the largest being reserved for the carrots, celery, broccoli, and tomatoes. Use one small compartment or bowl each for the hummus, ranch, cheese, and nuts.

HYPERION FINGER-GUN SANDWICHES

"Pewpewpew," then "chewchewchew"

In my brief time aboard Helios, I observed a corporate culture best described as sophomoric. Rather, it could be described as such if I believed any of the Hyperion rank and file knew what the word *sophomoric* meant. However, the general obsession with pretending their hands could become firearms made some sense; my hands actually *can* become firearms, and it is an extremely useful skill for dealing with the bandits and skags that call Pandora home. I created this dish so that the workers could have a nice treat between all their playacting. And worry not, adult children, for I have already cut the crusts off as well.

TIME: 15 minutes

YIELD: Serves 4

DIFFICULTY: Easy

- 4 ounces cold Brie
- 8 slices thin-cut white sandwich bread
- 4 teaspoons whole grain mustard
- 4 teaspoons fig jam
- 4 slices ham, preferably jambon de Paris (about 4 ounces)

1. While the Brie is cold, cut it into thin slices. Set aside, lightly covered, for 10 minutes.

2. Spread 1 teaspoon of whole grain mustard on four slices of bread. Spread 1 teaspoon of fig jam on the remaining bread slices.

3. Divide the sliced Brie among the four mustard-covered slices of bread. Cover the Brie with a slice of ham, followed by the jam-coated slices of bread.

4. With a very sharp knife, trim off the crusts of the sandwiches. (Feel free to snack on these or discard them.)

5. Working one at a time, cut each sandwich into two "gun" or L shapes. The easiest way to do this is to picture a 3-by-3 grid on top of the sandwich, then make four cuts to remove the middle square of the grid (two long cuts and two short cuts). The barrel of the "gun" should be about two-thirds the length of the sandwich, with the butt/handle of the gun being the remaining third. The remaining center square of the sandwich can be cut in half to be the "bullets," or you can just eat them.

6. Repeat with the remaining sandwiches and serve.

JANEY'S SPRINGS SALAD

An emporium of green stuff

ACCESSING ECHO LOG. SUBJECT: JANEY SPRINGS INTERVIEW

"Going 'round finding recipes, what a nice way to spend your time! I tell ya, most of the people that come through here, it's all bullets, treasure, and psychotic ramblings, but we've all gotta eat, don't we? Well, I'm happy to help, though I don't have anything too fancy. When I was still up on Elpis, I had a little garden, which was hard to keep going, what with being on a harsh, unforgiving moon and all. Still, I managed to put together a pretty bonza salad when harvest time came 'round, and I'm sure you'll be able to fancy it up plenty!"

TIME: 15 minutes

YIELD: Serves 4

DIETARY: Gluten free, Nondairy, Vegan

DIFFICULTY: Easy

FOR THE DRESSING
- 1 small shallot, finely minced
- ¼ cup fresh lemon juice
- 1 teaspoon Dijon mustard
- 1 small clove garlic, grated
- ¼ teaspoon kosher salt
- ½ cup extra-virgin olive oil

FOR THE SALAD
- 1 cup fresh spring peas
- 12 spears young asparagus, cut into 1-inch pieces
- 4 cups mixed spring greens, rinsed and drained
- 4 medium radishes, thinly sliced
- ¼ cup fresh dill, roughly chopped
- ¼ cup fresh mint leaves
- 4 ounces goat cheese, crumbled

TO MAKE THE DRESSING:
1. In a small bowl, whisk together the shallot, lemon juice, mustard, garlic, and salt until smooth and the salt has dissolved. While whisking constantly, add the oil in a very small, steady stream. Cover and chill until ready to use. (You can also put all the ingredients in a small glass jar and shake vigorously until emulsified.) Dressing can be made up to 1 week in advance.

TO MAKE THE SALAD:
2. Fill a bowl with 2 cups each of ice and water. Bring a medium pot of salted water to a boil over high heat. Add the peas and asparagus and blanch until bright green (1 to 2 minutes). Drain and transfer to the bowl of ice water. Let sit for a few minutes to cool completely, then drain.

3. In a large bowl, gently toss the mixed greens, radishes, dill, and mint leaves until evenly distributed. Toss in the asparagus and peas. Top with goat cheese and serve with the dressing.

EYE(S) OF THE DESTROYER

An Eye for taste

Pandora is a funny little world. On many planets, a dish styled after the eye of a world-ending nightmare beast would arguably be in bad taste. On Pandora, however, the typical response is disappointment that this dish is not a chance to eat the actual eye of a world-ending nightmare beast and gain its extradimensional power. In either case, my puff pastries are light and fluffy enough to overcome any misgivings.

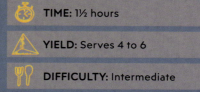

TIME: 1½ hours

YIELD: Serves 4 to 6

DIFFICULTY: Intermediate

- 1 sheet puff pastry, thawed
- 1 large egg
- 1 tablespoon water
- ¼ cup packed baby spinach leaves
- 4 slices prosciutto
- ½ cup aged Gouda, shredded
- ½ cup Manchego, shredded
- 24 canned black olive slices

1. Line two half-sheet pans with parchment paper. Roll the thawed puff pastry out to a 12-by-14-inch rectangle on a lightly floured surface.

2. In a small bowl, beat together the egg and water. Brush the puff pastry all over with the egg wash. Leaving a 1-inch border at one of the shorter edges, place the spinach leaves down in a single layer on the puff pastry.

3. Lay the prosciutto slices over the spinach, followed by the shredded cheeses. Starting at the short side without the clean border, roll the pastry and filling into a tight spiral, similar to a jelly roll. Pinch the seam to seal, then wrap the roll in plastic wrap. Freeze for 30 minutes.

4. Place oven racks at the upper and lower third positions, then preheat the oven to 400°F. Unwrap the puff pastry roll and transfer it to a cutting board. Cut into twenty-four ½-inch slices. Divide the slices between the two prepared sheet pans, laying them flat on their side.

5. Brush the tops of each slice with the remaining egg wash, then gently press an olive slice into the center of each spiral. Bake until puffed and golden for 15 to 20 minutes, swapping the positions of the pans about halfway through.

6. Transfer the cooked pinwheels to a wire rack to cool for 10 minutes before serving.

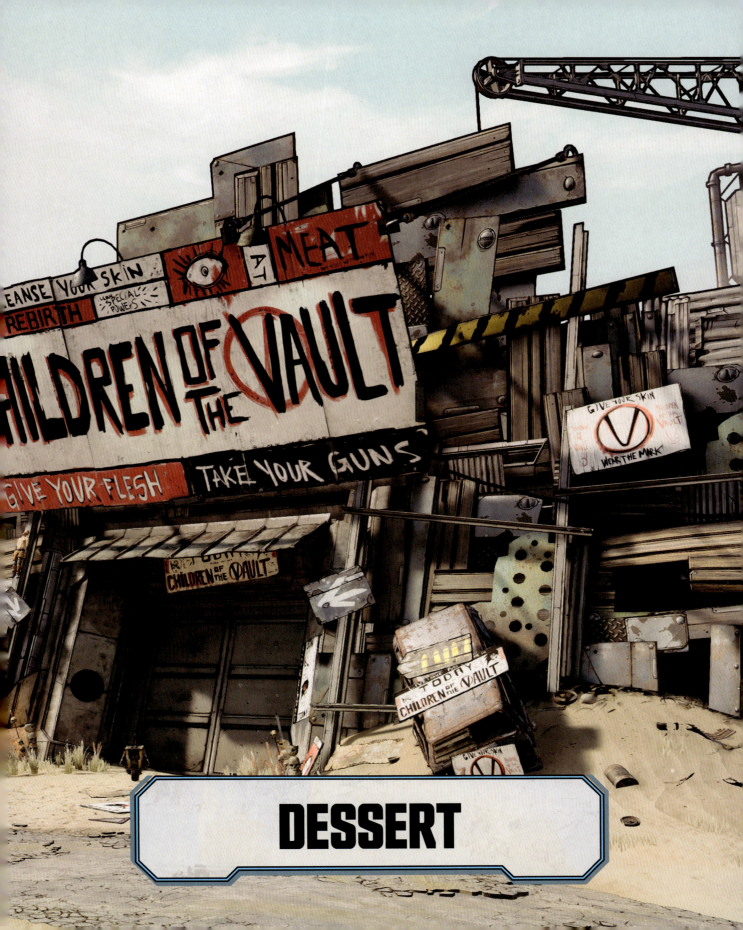

DESSERT

AXTON'S "WHEN LIFE GIVES YOU LEMONS" BARS

Revenge is a dish best served zesty

ACCESSING ECHO LOG. SUBJECT: AXTON'S RAMBLINGS

"You know the saying 'when life gives you lemons, make lemonade,' right? Why's lemonade the go-to thing to make? There are so many things you can do with a good lemon! Better things, arguably, and because I'm the guy with the sentry turret, I think I'm going to win the argument. Lemon bars, for example: now, *there's* a good use of lemons. So, in this scenario, bandits blowing up my Runner and leaving me stranded in the wastes? That'd be the lemons. Me getting revenge on your whole gang with this little ambush? Well, let's just call you Lemon Bar, pal."

TIME: 5½ hours
YIELD: 12 bars
DIETARY: Vegetarian
DIFFICULTY: Intermediate

FOR THE CRUST
- 1½ cups all-purpose flour
- ¼ cup granulated sugar
- 1 tablespoon cornstarch
- 1 teaspoon lemon zest
- 2 teaspoons ground ginger
- 1 teaspoon ground coriander
- ½ teaspoon kosher salt
- 8 tablespoons unsalted butter, cubed

FOR THE FILLING
- 1 cup granulated sugar
- 1 tablespoon lemon zest
- ¼ teaspoon kosher salt
- 3 large eggs
- 2 large egg yolks
- ½ cup fresh lemon juice

TO SERVE
- Powdered sugar

TO MAKE THE CRUST:

1. Preheat the oven to 325°F. Line a 9-by-9-inch baking pan with parchment paper so there's a 2- to 3-inch overhang on two of the sides.

2. In a food processor, pulse the flour, granulated sugar, cornstarch, lemon zest, ginger, coriander, salt, and butter until the mixture resembles coarse, wet sand. Tip into the prepared baking pan and press into an even layer on the bottom of the pan. (It's okay if the crust goes up the sides a bit, but the crust doesn't need to go up the sides completely.) Press the crust down with the bottom of a flat glass or measuring cup. Bake for 30 to 35 minutes, or until light golden.

TO MAKE THE FILLING:

3. In a small saucepan, whisk together the granulated sugar, lemon zest, salt, eggs, yolks, and lemon juice. Place over medium heat and cook, stirring constantly, until thickened and bubbling. Once you see the first bubbles hit the surface, continue stirring for about 30 seconds and then remove from the heat.

TO MAKE THE LEMON BARS AND SERVE:

4. Pour the lemon curd into a small bowl through a fine-mesh strainer. Discard any solids, then pour the curd over the prepared crust. Bake for 35 to 40 minutes, until the very center of the curd jiggles slightly when you shake the baking pan. Let cool to room temperature, then cover and chill for 4 hours.

5. Use the ends of the parchment paper to lift the lemon bars out of the pan and onto a cutting board. Dust generously with powdered sugar, then cut and serve.

ERIDIAN ÉCLAIRS

From the Vault of the Pastry Chef

It has become clear from my time on Pandora just how important the Eridian culture and its artifacts are to the people here. From countless scavenged alien weapons to the mysterious eridium that has caused many conflicts, no life in the galaxy is untouched by the memory of this lost race. So why should mealtimes be any different? Just as a Vault Hunter ends their long adventure with the treasure of a Vault, now you can end your dinner in the blue-tinted bounty of this Eridian-inspired pastry. This éclair is likely far less deadly than opening a Vault as well. This being Pandora, though, I make no promises.

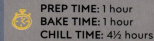

PREP TIME: 1 hour
BAKE TIME: 1 hour
CHILL TIME: 4½ hours

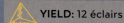

YIELD: 12 éclairs

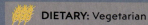

DIETARY: Vegetarian

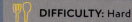

DIFFICULTY: Hard

FOR THE BLUEBERRY CURD
- 2 cups blueberries
- ¼ cup lemon juice
- 1 teaspoon ground coriander
- 1 cup granulated sugar
- 4 large eggs
- 8 tablespoons butter

FOR THE CHOUX PASTRY
- 1 cup whole milk
- 6 tablespoons unsalted butter
- 1 tablespoon granulated sugar
- ¾ teaspoon kosher salt
- 1 cup all-purpose flour, sifted
- 4 large eggs

TO MAKE THE BLUEBERRY CURD:

1. In a small saucepan, cook the blueberries and lemon juice over medium heat, stirring and mashing the blueberries frequently until they burst and release their juices (about 15 minutes).

2. Set a fine-mesh strainer over a heatproof bowl and pour the blueberry mixture through, pressing with the back of a spoon or rubber spatula. You should end up with ¾ cup of juice. (If you have considerably more, discard the excess or reserve it for another purpose.)

3. Rinse out the small saucepan and return the blueberry juice to it along with the coriander, granulated sugar, eggs, and butter. Cook over medium heat, stirring constantly, until thickened and bubbling. Once you see the first bubbles, set a 1-minute timer and continue to stir constantly. Remove from the heat, strain into a bowl, cover, and chill for 4 hours.

TO MAKE THE CHOUX PASTRY:

4. In a medium saucier, bring the milk, butter, granulated sugar, and salt to a boil over high heat. (If you don't have a saucier, a regular saucepan works just fine!) Remove from the heat and vigorously stir in the flour with a wooden spoon until smooth.

5. Return the saucier to high heat and continue stirring vigorously until the mixture reaches an internal temperature of 170°F.

6. Dump the mixture into the bowl of a stand mixer fitted with a paddle attachment. Beat on medium heat until the temperature drops to 145°F or lower. Start taking the temperature after about 3 minutes, then continue beating for 1 minute at a time until the correct temperature is reached.

RECIPE CONTINUES ON NEXT SPREAD.

FOR THE ICING
- 1 cup powdered sugar
- 1 teaspoon lemon zest
- 1 tablespoon light corn syrup
- 1 teaspoon vanilla extract
- 2 to 3 tablespoons heavy cream
- 3 to 6 drops electric-blue gel food coloring

7. Add the eggs one at a time, beating at medium speed until fully incorporated before adding the next egg. Once all the eggs are in, stop the mixer, scrape down the sides, and beat on medium speed for another 5 to 10 seconds until fully mixed.

8. Preheat the oven to 400°F. Line a half-sheet pan with parchment.

9. Transfer the choux batter to a large piping bag fitted with a large star tip. To keep the parchment from moving as you work, pipe a small blob of choux pastry under all four corners of the parchment.

10. Pipe twelve 4-by-1½-inch logs onto the parchment. Bake for 30 minutes, until the éclairs are a deep golden brown and well puffed. Turn off the oven and prop open the door with a wooden spoon, allowing the éclairs to sit for another 30 minutes in the warm oven. Transfer the éclairs to a wire rack to cool completely.

TO MAKE THE ICING:

11. In a small bowl, whisk together the powdered sugar, lemon zest, corn syrup, vanilla, 2 tablespoons of heavy cream, and the gel food coloring until smooth. If the mixture is too thick, add 1 additional teaspoon of heavy cream at a time until the desired consistency is reached. The icing should be very thick and flow very, very slowly. It should be thin enough to dip the éclairs in but thick enough that it doesn't run down the sides of the éclairs before it sets.

TO MAKE THE ÉCLAIRS:

12. Whisk the blueberry curd until smooth. Transfer to a piping bag fitted with a long filling tip. Insert the tip into one end of the éclair and pipe in the filling until you can just feel the éclair begin to expand. Be careful not to overfill or the éclairs may split—work slowly and carefully. If necessary, insert the tip into the opposite end to finish filling the éclair.

13. Repeat this process until all the éclairs are filled. Dip the tops of the éclairs into the icing and let the excess drip off for 10 seconds or so. If necessary, fill in any gaps with the icing using your finger or an offset spatula. Transfer the éclairs to a platter and chill, letting the icing set for 20 to 30 minutes before serving. Keep chilled in a sealed container and serve cold.

TINY TINA'S CHOCOLATE CHIP COOKIES

Exploding with chocolaty goodness!

ACCESSING ECHO LOG. SUBJECT: TINY TINA'S PERSONAL LOG, ENTRY #131

"It's game night, baby! Our first one in a while, too, so the best, most talented host in the known universe—that would be yours truly, duh—is doing it up right by making chocolate chip cookies. With all that intense gaming action, you need the best junk food you can get, and my cookies blow all other cookies out of the water! Seriously, other cookies, don't even bother stepping to me, I will blow you up! My cookies are only supposed to be the bomb metaphorically, but I will make them the bomb literally. DO NOT TEST ME!"

TIME: 2 hours

YIELD: About 3 dozen

DIETARY: Vegetarian

DIFFICULTY: Easy

- 16 tablespoons unsalted butter
- 1 cup dark brown sugar
- ½ cup granulated sugar
- 1½ teaspoons kosher salt
- ¾ teaspoon baking soda
- 1 pinch freshly grated nutmeg
- 2 large eggs
- 1 large egg yolk
- 1 tablespoon vanilla extract
- 2 cups all-purpose flour
- 1½ cups dark chocolate chips

1. In a small saucepan, cook the butter over medium heat, swirling and stirring with a rubber spatula, until the butter smells nutty and you can see little golden-brown bits at the bottom of the pan (5 to 7 minutes).

2. Pour the butter into a heatproof bowl. Add the brown sugar, granulated sugar, and salt. Beat with an electric mixer until smooth (2 to 4 minutes). Add the baking soda, nutmeg, and one of the eggs. Beat until smooth, about 1 minute, then add the remaining egg and yolk, beating for 1 minute between each addition. Beat in the vanilla.

3. Stir in the flour and chocolate chips and mix until just incorporated and no dry flour remains. Cover the bowl and chill for at least 1 hour (up to 4 days). The longer you let the dough chill, the more the flavors will meld and develop.

4. Preheat the oven to 350°F. Line a half-sheet pan with parchment paper. Use a 2-tablespoon cookie scoop (or a rounded 1-tablespoon measure) to portion the dough into 12 cookies, spacing them evenly on the prepared pan. Cover and chill the remaining dough until you're ready to bake the next batch.

5. Bake the cookies until golden brown at the edges and barely set in the centers (10 to 13 minutes). Let cool on the pan for 5 minutes before transferring to a wire rack to cool completely. Repeat the process with the remaining dough. Store baked cookies in a sealed container at room temperature for up to 3 days. The dough can be portioned out and stored in a zipper-top bag in the freezer for up to 3 months. You can bake from frozen (adding a few minutes to the total bake time) or thaw before baking.

CLAPTRAP'S BIRTHDAY CAKE FOR ONE

A single serving for a single sad sack

After some reflection, I have to admit to feeling a *little* bad for Claptrap. Yes, he is endlessly annoying, but even the most insufferable among us deserves a win every now and then. So, as a glad gesture for this sad jester, I have made a birthday cake fitting his solitary status. I realize that, as a robot, he cannot eat it, but food is kind of my whole thing, and it really should be the thought that counts.

TIME: 1½ hours
YIELD: Serves 2 (1 imaginary)
DIETARY: Vegetarian
DIFFICULTY: Intermediate

FOR THE CAKE
- 1 tablespoon unsalted butter, softened
- 2 large egg whites
- 3 tablespoons granulated sugar
- 2 tablespoons neutral oil, such as canola or safflower
- 2 teaspoons vanilla extract
- ½ cup cake flour, sifted
- ¼ teaspoon baking powder
- ¼ teaspoon kosher salt
- 2 tablespoons buttermilk
- 2 tablespoons sprinkles

TO MAKE THE CAKE:
1. Use the butter to grease the bottom and sides of two 4-ounce ramekins. Line the bottoms of each with a small circle of parchment paper. Set the ramekins on a half- or quarter-sheet pan.

2. In a medium bowl using an electric mixer, beat together the egg whites, granulated sugar, oil, and vanilla on medium speed until smooth and slightly thickened (about 2 minutes).

3. In a small bowl, sift together the flour, baking powder, and salt. Add half of this mixture to the bowl with the egg white mixture. Beat on low until just incorporated, then beat in the buttermilk. Beat in the remaining flour, then fold in the sprinkles.

4. Divide the cake batter between the two prepared ramekins. Place in a cold oven (see note), then set the oven to 325°F. Bake for 30 to 35 minutes, until a toothpick inserted into the center of the cakes comes out mostly clean with a few moist crumbs clinging to it.

5. Transfer the ramekins to a wire rack to cool until you're able to safely handle them, then invert to remove the cakes (use a thin paring knife to loosen from the sides of the ramekins if necessary). Set the cakes on a wire rack to cool completely.

RECIPE CONTINUES ON NEXT SPREAD.

FOR THE FROSTING
- » 4 tablespoons unsalted butter, softened
- » 1 cup powdered sugar, sifted
- » ¼ teaspoon kosher salt
- » 1 teaspoon vanilla extract
- » 1 teaspoon lemon zest
- » 1 to 2 tablespoons lemon juice
- » ¼ teaspoon electric-yellow gel food coloring (optional)

TO DECORATE
- » 1 tablespoon sprinkles
- » 1 candle

TO MAKE THE FROSTING:

6. In a large bowl using an electric mixer, beat the butter on high speed until soft and creamy (about 3 minutes). Turn off the mixer, then add the powdered sugar, salt, vanilla, and lemon zest. Beat on low until moistened, then gradually increase the speed to high until the frosting begins to come together. Add 1 tablespoon of lemon juice and beat until creamy (about 5 minutes). If the frosting is quite thick, add another teaspoon of lemon juice (or more as needed). The frosting should be light, fluffy, and easily spreadable but still hold its shape. Beat in the food coloring, if using.

TO ASSEMBLE AND DECORATE:

7. Trim off the domed tops of both cakes with a serrated knife so they are level. Cut both cakes horizontally into two even layers, for a total of four layers. Save the bottoms of both cakes to be the bottom and top of the finished cake (the bottom layer will be cut-side up and the top layer will be cut-side down).

8. Place the bottom layer of the cake on a platter or cake decorating stand. Spread about 1 tablespoon of frosting in an even layer on top. Place the second layer on top, followed by another 1 tablespoon of frosting spread evenly. Add the third layer, another 1 tablespoon of frosting spread evenly, followed by the final layer of cake.

9. Use the remaining frosting to coat the entire outside of the cake. Decorate the top and sides with more sprinkles.

NOTE: It's important to start this in a cold oven so the ramekins heat up with the oven and slowly bake the cake. The result is a springy but tender cake that's easy to decorate.

ERIDI-YUM-YUMS

Upgrade your snack pack today!

The people of Pandora have found many genuine uses for eridium, so it's alarming how many of the planet's less mentally stable citizens continue to try eating the stuff to, quote, "absorb the unknown powers of the past [extended maniacal laughter]" unquote. Explaining that eridium's high toxicity will only lead to agonizing death does little to dissuade anyone. Though I am nobody's mother, I felt obligated to create a visually similar alternative that is not only edible, but will at worst just give them a sugar high. A bandit on a sugar high is its own terrifying thought, but I've at least solved the first problem.

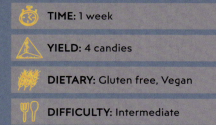

TIME: 1 week

YIELD: 4 candies

DIETARY: Gluten free, Vegan

DIFFICULTY: Intermediate

- 6 cups granulated sugar
- 2 cups water
- ½ teaspoon gel food coloring (your choice of color)
- 1 teaspoon artificial or natural flavor extract (optional)

1. Wash out a 1-quart canning jar with very hot water and soap. Rinse well and let dry.

2. Dip the pointed ends of four wooden skewers in water, then dip in the granulated sugar you're using in this recipe. Set aside on a clean plate until ready to use. This will provide a foundation for the crystals to build upon.

3. Pour 2 cups of water into a large saucepan. Bring to a boil over high heat, then add 1 cup of sugar. Stir until dissolved, then add another cup of sugar. Repeat this process, making sure each cup of sugar is completely dissolved before adding the next, until all the sugar is added and the mixture is slightly thick.

4. Remove the pan from the heat and stir in the gel food coloring, followed by the flavor extract (if using). Pour into the prepared jar. Let cool to room temperature before proceeding to the next step.

5. Dip the skewers (sugared-side first) into the sugar solution, then use clothespins or chip clips to suspend them so that the tips of the skewers are about 1 inch from the bottom of the jar. You can do this by resting the clips on the rim of the jar or by first topping the jar with a metal or plastic lid that you've punched holes in (then use the clips to keep the skewers from sliding all the way down).

6. Place the jar in a safe spot where it won't be moved for the next week. Check back every day to see the crystals start to form. After about a week, carefully remove the clips and lid (the skewers will likely stay in place, as the crystals on the skewers and the crystals on the bottom of the jar tend to fuse together). Break apart the crystals that have formed at the top of the jar, then carefully wiggle each skewer to release them from the bottom of the jar.

ANGEL'S ANGEL FOOD CAKE

Aka Siren's snack cakes

Following the destruction of Helios, countless fragmented digital files from its internal network leaked onto the ECHOnet. As a chef, I've only cared about decoding data that might lead to a new dish or two. In my research, I came across this angel food cake recipe, scrubbed from Handsome Jack's personal accounts. Knowing the rumors around his daughter, Angel, and his questionable treatment of her, I have no idea if he truly cared about her one way or the other. Whatever the case, he did have this dessert marked as "my Angel's favorite." Make of that what you will.

TIME: 3 hours 15 minutes

YIELD: Serves 8 to 12

DIETARY: Vegetarian

DIFFICULTY: Intermediate

FOR THE CAKE
- 1 cup cake flour, sifted three times
- 1 cup granulated sugar, divided
- 12 large egg whites
- 2 tablespoons lemon juice
- ½ teaspoon cream of tartar
- 1 tablespoon vanilla extract
- ½ teaspoon kosher salt
- 1 teaspoon lemon zest

TO ASSEMBLE
- 1 pound strawberries, hulled and sliced
- ¼ cup granulated sugar
- 1 tablespoon balsamic vinegar
- Whipped cream, to serve

TO MAKE THE CAKE:

1. Preheat the oven to 350°F. In a small bowl, sift together the cake flour and ¼ cup of granulated sugar. Set aside.

2. In the bowl of a stand mixer fitted with the whisk attachment, whisk the egg whites on medium-low speed until frothy, then add the lemon juice, cream of tartar, vanilla, salt, and lemon zest.

3. Increase the speed of the mixer to medium, then add the remaining ¾ cup of sugar a little at a time until it's all incorporated. Increase the speed of the mixer to medium-high and beat until very soft peaks form (3 to 5 minutes). Remove the bowl from the mixer and shake and scrape the excess meringue from the whisk attachment into the bowl.

4. Sprinkle the cake flour mixture all over the top of the meringue, then use a rubber spatula to gently fold the flour into the meringue. Keep folding until there are no more patches of dry flour left in the mixture.

5. Pour the cake batter into a clean, ungreased 10-inch tube pan with feet and a removable bottom. Smooth the batter to an even layer, then bake until puffed and golden (40 to 45 minutes).

6. Invert the cake pan on a heatproof surface and let it cool for about 2 hours, until it reaches room temperature. (Cooling it this way prevents the cake from collapsing.)

TO ASSEMBLE THE CAKE:

7. While the cake cools, in a medium bowl, toss together the strawberries, granulated sugar, and the balsamic vinegar. Let sit at room temperature, covered, tossing every 15 minutes or so, until the cake is cool. This process, known as macerating, makes the strawberries softer and draws out their natural juices to make a syrup.

8. Flip the cake pan back over so the cake is facing up. Loosen the cake from the sides of the pan by running a thin, sharp paring knife all around the edge of the cake. Grip the tube and gently lift the cake out of the pan. Run the knife along the bottom of the cake and the outside of the tube to loosen it from the base of the pan, then invert on a plate. Slice and serve with the macerated strawberries and whipped cream. Keep the leftover strawberries in a sealed container in the fridge for up to 3 days. Keep the leftover cake wrapped tightly at room temperature for up to 3 days.

TINY TINA'S LEAST-FAVORITE OATMEAL RAISIN COOKIES

I'll tell you what's raisin' . . . my frustration level!

ACCESSING ECHO LOG. SUBJECT: TINY TINA'S PERSONAL LOG, ENTRY #132

"Aggggh, last night was almost a total disaster! Why, you ask, nosy ECHO recorder? Because the store was sold out of chocolate chips! What?! What are you trying to do to me?! And can you believe the shopkeeper tried to suggest oatmeal raisin as an alternative? Tell me all the bombs I left behind weren't justified. YOU CAN'T DO IT! Still, I wasn't going to NOT have cookies at game night, and dumb as oatmeal raisin might be, people seemed to not entirely hate mine. Proof of just how excellenterrific I am that I could make them work. So the game was saved! And whenever they finish rebuilding it, the store now knows to always keep chocolate chips in stock, so double-win for Tina!"

TIME: 45 minutes

YIELD: About 3 dozen

DIETARY: Vegetarian

DIFFICULTY: Easy

- 16 tablespoons unsalted butter, softened
- 1½ cups dark brown sugar
- 1 teaspoon kosher salt
- 1 teaspoon baking soda
- 1½ teaspoons ground cinnamon
- ½ teaspoon ground ginger
- 1 pinch freshly grated nutmeg
- 2 large eggs
- 1 tablespoon vanilla extract
- 1½ cups all-purpose flour
- 2½ cups rolled oats
- 2 cups raisins

1. Preheat the oven to 350°F. Line a half-sheet pan with parchment paper.
2. In a large bowl using an electric mixer, beat the butter on high speed for 3 minutes, until smooth and creamy. Add the brown sugar, salt, baking soda, cinnamon, ginger, and nutmeg and beat until smooth, lightened in color, and fluffy (5 to 7 minutes).
3. Beat in the eggs one at a time, beating for 1 minute, until smooth. Beat in the vanilla. Add the flour and beat on low speed until just incorporated. Use a wooden spoon or rubber spatula to stir in the oats and raisins.
4. Use a 2-tablespoon cookie scoop (or a rounded 1-tablespoon measure) to portion the dough into 12 cookies, spacing them evenly on the prepared pan. Cover and chill the remaining dough until you're ready to bake the next batch.
5. Bake until the edges are golden brown and the centers are just set (10 to 13 minutes). Cool for 5 minutes on the pan, then transfer to a wire rack to cool completely. Repeat the process with the remaining dough. Keep cookies in a sealed container at room temperature for up to 3 days. The dough can be portioned out and stored in a zipper-top bag in the freezer for up to 3 months. You can bake from frozen (adding a few minutes to the total bake time) or thaw before baking.

NOTE: Oatmeal cookies typically bake well from frozen, but sometimes the oats can absorb too much moisture, and this can mess up the consistency or prevent the cookie from spreading. If you want to freeze the dough but find that the cookies afterward are dry, there are a few remedies you can try. First, you can lower the temperature and cook longer. Alternatively, you can let the frozen dough sit out at room temperature for 10 to 15 minutes and flatten them a bit before baking. Lastly, you can try using frozen butter instead of softened butter, which will help keep the oats from absorbing it.

BRICK'S POUND CAKE

A Slab King of sweetness

Few denizens of Pandora can match the raw physical strength of Brick, a fact I can personally attest to after seeing him in action. What better tribute to a man that pounds his enemies into submission than a pound cake? Still, even though this dessert packs a punch of flavor, it is nowhere near as dense or hefty as the furious fists belonging to the one they call the Slab King. This was proven when Brick took the name a little too literally and slammed his fist into my first serving of pound cake . . . and through the table I'd put it on.

TIME: 1 hour 15 minutes

YIELD: Serves 8 to 12

DIETARY: Vegetarian

DIFFICULTY: Easy

- 16 tablespoons unsalted butter, softened, plus more for greasing
- 1 cup granulated sugar
- ¼ cup honey
- 1 tablespoon lemon zest
- 1 teaspoon kosher salt
- ½ teaspoon baking powder
- 6 large eggs, room temperature
- 1 tablespoon vanilla extract
- 2 cups all-purpose flour

1. Preheat the oven to 350°F. Generously grease a 9-by-5-inch loaf pan with butter.
2. In a large bowl using an electric mixer, cream together the butter, granulated sugar, honey, lemon zest, salt, and baking powder on high speed until light and fluffy (5 to 7 minutes). Reduce the speed to medium, then add the eggs, one at a time, beating for 1 minute between each addition. Beat in the vanilla.
3. Turn mixer off, then add the flour. Beat on low until fully incorporated. Scrape the batter into the prepared pan, then bake until golden brown (50 to 60 minutes). A toothpick inserted into the center of the cake should come out mostly clean, with just a few moist crumbs clinging to it.
4. Let the cake cool in the pan for 10 to 15 minutes, then transfer to a wire cooling rack to cool completely before serving. Store tightly wrapped at room temperature for up to 4 days.

GAIGE'S ANARCHY APPLE PIE

Chaos in the kitchen

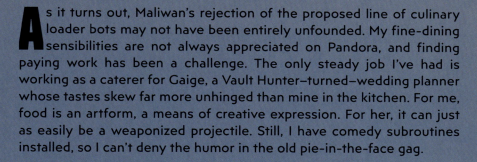

As it turns out, Maliwan's rejection of the proposed line of culinary loader bots may not have been entirely unfounded. My fine-dining sensibilities are not always appreciated on Pandora, and finding paying work has been a challenge. The only steady job I've had is working as a caterer for Gaige, a Vault Hunter–turned–wedding planner whose tastes skew far more unhinged than mine in the kitchen. For me, food is an artform, a means of creative expression. For her, it can just as easily be a weaponized projectile. Still, I have comedy subroutines installed, so I can't deny the humor in the old pie-in-the-face gag.

TIME: 3 hours 45 minutes
YIELD: Serves 8
DIETARY: Vegetarian
DIFFICULTY: Easy

FOR THE PIECRUST
- 1 cup all-purpose flour
- ½ cup rye flour
- ½ teaspoon kosher salt
- 2 teaspoons granulated sugar
- 8 tablespoons cold, unsalted butter, cubed
- 3 tablespoons ice-cold water

FOR THE HOMEMADE CRANBERRY SAUCE
- One 12-ounce bag fresh or frozen cranberries
- ¾ cup granulated sugar
- 1 cinnamon stick
- ¼ cup orange juice
- 1 tablespoon orange zest

FOR THE APPLE FILLING
- 2 large, tart apples, such as Granny Smith, cored and thinly sliced
- ¼ cup light brown sugar, lightly packed
- 2 teaspoons ground cinnamon
- 2 tablespoons tapioca starch
- 1 tablespoon lemon juice
- ¼ cup homemade cranberry sauce

TO MAKE THE PIECRUST:

1. In a food processor, pulse the all-purpose flour, rye flour, salt, and granulated sugar to combine, then add the butter. Pulse until the mixture resembles coarse, wet sand with some larger, pea-size pieces of butter throughout (1 to 2 minutes).

2. Tip the contents of the food processor into a medium bowl. Add the water and, working quickly with your hands, mix to form a rough dough with no patches of dry flour. Remove a golf ball–size piece of dough, shape into a disk, wrap with plastic wrap, and chill. Shape the remaining dough into a disk, wrap with plastic wrap, and chill for at least 2 hours.

TO MAKE THE HOMEMADE CRANBERRY SAUCE:

3. In a medium saucepan, combine the cranberries, granulated sugar, cinnamon stick, orange juice, and orange zest. Bring to a boil over high heat, then reduce to medium. Cook, stirring constantly, until the cranberries have burst and the sauce has reduced to a thick, jammy consistency (10 to 15 minutes). Transfer to a heatproof container, cover, and chill for 2 hours. (This can be done a few days ahead of time.)

TO MAKE THE APPLE FILLING:

4. Just before you're ready to assemble, add the apples to a large bowl. Toss with the brown sugar, cinnamon, tapioca starch, lemon juice, and the chilled cranberry sauce.

RECIPE CONTINUES ON NEXT SPREAD.

TO ASSEMBLE
- 1 large egg
- 1 tablespoon water
- Raw sugar, for sprinkling

TO ASSEMBLE AND BAKE:

5. Line a half-sheet pan with parchment paper. Roll out the larger disk of dough on a lightly floured work surface to a thickness of about ⅛ inch. The dough should end up as a round, sort of oval shape with ragged edges—don't worry about perfection here. Transfer the dough to the prepared sheet pan, and don't worry if the edges of the dough hang over the sides of the pan.

6. Spread the cranberry sauce in an even layer in the middle of the dough, leaving a 2-inch border of bare dough around the sauce. Spread the apple filling over the cranberry sauce. If you feel the need for order (very unanarchistic of you), feel free to arrange the apple slices in a scalloped, decorative spiral. Fold the bare border over the apple filling, adding a pleat every 4 inches or so. Transfer the pan to the freezer.

7. Roll out the smaller disk of dough on a lightly floured surface to a thickness of roughly ¼ inch. Use a toothpick or the tip of a paring knife to draw an anarchy symbol in the dough using ¼-inch-thick lines. Transfer the dough to a plate or small cutting board. Cut away the negative space, working carefully. Transfer to the freezer and let freeze for 15 minutes until the dough is firm enough to pull away the cutouts without ruining the lines of the symbol. Discard the cutouts and transfer the symbol to the prepared pan, next to the galette. If you don't have space for the symbol, transfer to a small, parchment-lined half- or quarter-sheet pan.

8. Preheat the oven to 400°F. In a small bowl, beat the egg and water together. Brush the crust of the galette and the anarchy symbol all over with the egg wash. Sprinkle generously with raw sugar. Bake for 35 to 45 minutes, until the crust is deep golden brown and the filling is bubbling. (The anarchy symbol only takes about 10 to 15 minutes to turn golden, so set a separate timer for it and transfer to a cooling rack with a thin spatula if baking on the same pan as the galette.)

9. Place the sheet pan on a wire cooling rack and let the galette cool for at least 20 minutes before transferring the anarchy symbol to the center. Slice and serve warm or at room temperature. Keep the leftover galette refrigerated and tightly wrapped for up to 3 days.

MECHROMANCER MUFFINS

More like MUFFIN-mancer, amirite?

For a brief period, I wondered if my culinary mission would be easier if I could teach other robotic individuals to cook as well. If my attempts to work with Claptrap weren't enough to dissuade me of this notion, then my time in the kitchen with DT put the final nail in the coffin. Though they were enthusiastic about making a dessert for Gaige, their murderous inclinations were a bad match for the delicate work of baking. I suppose, given that their name is Deathtrap, this one was on me. However, their incendiary death stare did prove useful in reaching optimal baking temperature after they destroyed my oven, so hope springs eternal.

TIME: 45 minutes
YIELD: 12 jumbo muffins
DIETARY: Vegetarian
DIFFICULTY: Easy

- 8 tablespoons unsalted butter, softened
- 1 cup granulated sugar
- ¾ teaspoon kosher salt
- 2 teaspoons baking powder
- 1 tablespoon vanilla extract
- 1 tablespoon red food coloring
- 2 large eggs, room temperature
- ½ cup buttermilk, room temperature
- 2 tablespoons apple cider vinegar
- 2 cups all-purpose flour
- 1 cup white chocolate chips
- 1 cup dark chocolate chips or chunks
- ¼ cup raw sugar

1. Preheat the oven to 350°F. Line two jumbo, 6-cup muffin pans with paper liners.
2. In a large bowl using an electric mixer, cream together the butter, granulated sugar, salt, baking powder, and vanilla on medium-high speed until smooth, light, and fluffy (5 to 7 minutes). Beat in the food coloring and one of the eggs for about 1 minute, mixing until the egg is incorporated. Beat in the remaining egg until incorporated.
3. In a small bowl or measuring cup, whisk together the buttermilk and vinegar. Set aside.
4. Beat half the flour into the butter mixture on low until just incorporated. Beat in the buttermilk mixture, followed by the remaining flour. Stir in the white and dark chocolate chips.
5. Divide the batter among the 12 muffin cups. Top each with about 1 teaspoon of raw sugar. Bake for 25 to 30 minutes, until a toothpick inserted into the center of a muffin comes out mostly clean with a few moist crumbs clinging to it.
6. Let the muffins cool in the pan for 5 minutes before transferring to a wire cooling rack to cool completely. Store leftover muffins at room temperature in a sealed container for up to 3 days.

ELLIE'S DUMP CAKE

Catch-a-slice!

It is generally my desire to make every recipe I present as appealing as possible, so I want to be clear that I fought Ellie on the name for this one. Yes, dump cakes are a dessert standard, but given Ellie's close association with scrapyards, I did not wish to imply this dessert was at all involved with an actual junkyard. For her part, Ellie simply found the idea extremely amusing, and as I owe her several times over for all the bullet holes she's patched up, the name stands. I promise, with this cake, you will taste blackberries and bourbon, not scorched metal and motor oil.

TIME: 55 minutes

YIELD: Serves 12 to 16

DIETARY: Vegetarian

DIFFICULTY: Easy

- 2 cans blackberry pie filling
- ¼ cup bourbon
- 1 teaspoon ground cinnamon
- One 15.25-ounce box yellow cake mix
- 12 tablespoons unsalted butter, melted
- 1 cup chopped pecans
- Whipped cream or vanilla ice cream, to serve

1. Preheat the oven to 350°F. Dump the blackberry pie filling, bourbon, and cinnamon into a 9-by-13-inch baking dish. Stir to combine.

2. Top the filling with the cake mix in an even layer. Drizzle all over with the melted butter. Top with chopped pecans. Bake for 40 to 45 minutes, until the top is golden brown and the filling is bubbling.

3. Let cool for 15 minutes before serving warm with whipped cream or vanilla ice cream (or both!). Keep the leftover cake covered and refrigerated for up to 3 days.

FRAN'S RED RIPPLE SURPRISE FROGURT

Go with the froyo flow

ACCESSING ECHO LOG. SUBJECT: FRAN MISCOWICZ INTERVIEW

"All right, you bucket of bolts, I guess you're on the level. And Octavio's always getting on me to explore new promotional opportunities, so I suppose Fran's Frogurt would be open to including one of our original flavors in your robotic beep-boop cookbook. But let's be clear, tin man, we'd best get our cut of any and all future profits. Trust me, I am not the sort of person you want to double-cross. After all"—[freeze ray charging]—"yogurt ain't the only thing I know how to put on ice."

TIME: 7 hours 45 minutes

YIELD: About 2 quarts

DIETARY: Gluten free, Vegetarian

DIFFICULTY: Intermediate

- 2 pounds strawberries, hulled and sliced
- 1½ cups granulated sugar
- 2 tablespoons berry-flavored vodka (plain vodka is also fine)
- 2 cups plain, unsweetened Greek yogurt
- 2 teaspoons vanilla extract
- Juice of ½ lemon
- ½ cup dark chocolate chips or chunks
- 2 teaspoons refined coconut oil

1. In a large bowl, toss together the strawberries, granulated sugar, and vodka. Cover and leave at room temperature for at least 1 hour and up to 3 hours, stirring every 20 minutes or so. This process, known as macerating, makes the strawberries softer and draws out their natural juices to make a syrup.

2. In a food processor, pulse the macerated strawberries, Greek yogurt, vanilla, and lemon juice until smooth. Strain through a fine-mesh strainer set over a bowl, stirring and pressing the mixture through with a rubber spatula. Discard any solids. Cover the bowl and chill for 4 hours (or up to 2 days).

3. In a microwave-safe bowl, microwave the chocolate chips and coconut oil in 30-second bursts, stirring each time, until smooth. Let cool slightly.

4. Using an ice-cream machine, churn the yogurt mixture according to your machine's instructions. During the few minutes of churning, add the chocolate mixture in a slow, steady stream. It will harden almost instantly and break apart as it gets churned into the frozen yogurt, creating a ripple of crisp chocolate throughout.

5. Scoop the churned frozen yogurt into freezer-safe containers and keep frozen for up to 3 months.

NOTE: The base may be too much for some ice-cream makers, as this yields about 2 quarts. You can either make this in batches or halve the recipe to make about 1 quart. Making it in batches will be easier if your ice-cream maker has a compressor and can make multiple batches consecutively. If you have the type that requires freezing the bowl overnight, this project will take multiple days.

Additionally, the frozen yogurt will have the consistency of soft serve right out of the machine and can be served right away, but any frozen yogurt you're not serving should be transferred to the freezer.

ROLAND'S CRIMSON BRAIDERS

Join the fight . . . against hunger!

When he was first assembling the Crimson Raiders, Roland understood he would need to show the soldiers abandoned by Atlas a new way. Not only did he present them with a common enemy in Hyperion, but he also showed them a true sense of community at their initial base in New Haven. This included weekly team-building events, many of which would end with a serving of braided sweetbread made to commemorate the man who'd brought them all together. It's enough to bring a tear to your optical lens.

TIME: 4 hours

YIELD: Serves 6 to 8

DIETARY: Vegetarian

DIFFICULTY: Hard

FOR THE DOUGH
- 2 cups bread flour
- 1 teaspoon kosher salt
- 2½ teaspoons instant yeast
- 1 tablespoon granulated sugar
- ½ cup lukewarm milk (any %)
- 1 large egg, room temperature, lightly beaten
- 4 tablespoons unsalted butter, softened, plus more for greasing

TO MAKE THE DOUGH:

1. In the bowl of a stand mixer fitted with the dough hook attachment, mix the flour and salt on low speed to combine, then add the yeast, granulated sugar, and milk. Mix until moistened, then add the egg and increase the speed to medium. Continue mixing for 5 to 7 minutes, until a shaggy dough forms.

2. Add the butter, 1 tablespoon at a time, allowing the butter to become fully incorporated before adding the next tablespoon. Once all the butter has been added, knead for about 15 minutes, until the dough is smooth, shiny, and elastic. The dough should pass the windowpane test (this is when you pull off a small piece of dough and stretch it between your fingers—you should be able to stretch it until you can just start to see through the dough without it tearing).

3. Transfer the dough to a lightly greased bowl or container and let rise for 1 hour, or until doubled in volume. Meanwhile, put the cherries and pomegranate juice in a bowl. Cover and let sit for 45 minutes.

TO MAKE THE FILLING:

4. Drain the cherries, discarding the juice. In a medium bowl using an electric mixer on high, beat the butter, brown sugar, and flour until smooth, light, and fluffy (about 5 minutes). Stir in the drained cherries, cranberries, pecans, and chocolate chips.

5. Line a half-sheet pan with parchment paper. Roll out the dough on a lightly floured surface to a roughly 11-by-14-inch rectangle. Rotate the dough so one of the long sides is facing you. Spread the filling in an even layer all over, leaving a 1-inch border at the long side opposite you.

118

FOR THE FILLING
- ¾ cup dried cherries, chopped
- ¾ cup pomegranate juice
- 8 tablespoons butter, softened
- ⅓ cup dark brown sugar
- ¼ cup all-purpose flour
- ¼ cup dried cranberries
- ½ cup chopped pecans
- ¼ cup mini chocolate chips

FOR THE ICING
- ¼ cup unsweetened cocoa powder
- ⅔ cup powdered sugar
- 1 pinch kosher salt
- 1 teaspoon vanilla
- 3 tablespoons heavy cream

6. Starting at the long side facing you, roll the dough into a tight coil, similar to a jelly roll, pinching the seam together tightly. Transfer the log to the prepared sheet pan. Using a sharp knife or bench scraper, cut the log in half lengthwise, leaving one end connected by about ½ inch of dough. Braid the two halves together, then create a loop by joining the two ends together.

7. Cover the dough with a lightly greased piece of plastic wrap. Let rise for about 1 hour, until well puffed and nearly doubled in volume. Toward the end of the rising time, preheat the oven to 400°F.

8. Bake for about 25 minutes, or until deep golden brown and an instant-read thermometer registers 200°F when inserted into the very center of the bread ring. Let cool in the pan for 10 minutes before transferring to a wire rack to cool completely.

TO MAKE THE ICING:

9. As the bread cools, sift the cocoa and powdered sugar together into a small bowl. Whisk in the salt, vanilla, and heavy cream until smooth. Drizzle over the cooled bread before slicing and serving. Bread can be kept tightly wrapped at room temperature for up to 2 days.

TORGUE'S PROTEIN SHAKE

"GET THOSE GAINS!" —Mr. Torgue

Mr. Torgue clearly believes in the idea of "more is more" in all aspects of his life. His protein shake is a nightmarish brew of ingredients, including coffee grounds, raw eggs, and a healthy amount of ground chuck to, and I quote, "PUT EVEN MORE BEEF ON THIS BEEFY BOD." I've cut all of that, both for health concerns and in pursuit of creating a drink that anyone other than the universe's most explosive CEO would dare to drink. Instead, I've stuck to the sweeter ingredients, which still pack plenty of protein to power up your pre-workout game.

TIME: 5 minutes

YIELD: 1 shake

DIETARY: Gluten free, Nondairy, Vegan

DIFFICULTY: Easy

- ¾ cup frozen banana chunks
- 3 or 4 dried dates, pitted
- ¼ cup plant-based, unsweetened, unflavored protein powder
- 1 tablespoon unsweetened cocoa powder
- 2 tablespoons peanut butter
- 1 cup unsweetened vanilla almond milk

1. In a blender, blend the frozen banana chunks, dates, protein powder, cocoa powder, peanut butter, and vanilla almond milk on low speed, then gradually increase the speed to high. Blend until smooth, about 2 minutes.
2. Pour into a 20-ounce glass and serve immediately.

LOR'S DOUBLE BARREL BREW

Espresso shot through the heart

I have a great appreciation for the calm of Promethea, especially after all the time I've spent dealing with the chaos of Pandora. When not under imminent threat of invasion—a more common problem than one might expect—the planet is downright idyllic, with more modern comforts than most of its planetary neighbors. A number of my favorite finds come from Meridian Metroplex's most popular coffee shop, and the owner, Lor, was happy to share one of his recipes with me. It's a truly delightful brew by all measures, one made even more impressive by Lor's ability to continue mixing up new drinks between all the freedom fighting.

TIME: 25 minutes

YIELD: 1 latte

DIETARY: Gluten free, Vegetarian

DIFFICULTY: Intermediate

FOR THE HONEY-LAVENDER SYRUP
- 1 cup water
- ½ cup honey
- ½ cup granulated sugar
- 1 vanilla bean
- 2 tablespoons dried culinary lavender buds

TO ASSEMBLE
- 2 shots espresso, hot (pulled fresh, or made from instant powder mix)
- 1 cup milk (any %)

TO MAKE THE HONEY-LAVENDER SYRUP:

1. In a small saucepan, combine the water, honey, and granulated sugar. Cut the vanilla bean in half lengthwise. Scrape out the seeds and add to the saucepan, along with the split vanilla bean pod and lavender buds. Bring to a boil over high heat, stirring until sugar and honey have dissolved, then remove from the heat, cover, and let steep for 15 minutes. Pour through a fine-mesh strainer set over a heatproof bowl.

TO ASSEMBLE:

2. Pour the espresso into a 12-ounce mug, along with 1 to 2 tablespoons of the honey lavender syrup. If you have an espresso machine with a milk steaming wand, steam and froth the milk according to the manufacturer's instructions. Otherwise, heat the milk in a small saucepan until just steaming and whisk vigorously with a milk frother or wire whisk before pouring over the espresso mixture. Serve hot.

NOTE: Syrup can be made well in advance and stored in the fridge in an airtight container for up to 1 month.

TEDIORE'S BRISK ACE TEA

Disrupting the iced-tea space

One of the strictest and most brutal chairwomen the Tediore corporation has ever seen, Susan Coldwell lives up to her own name with an icy disposition and a withering stare that chills her underlings to the bone. I've aimed to capture that frosty energy with this bracing mint tea mix, one that's sure to give you the energizing kick you need. I had hoped to ask some actual Tediore employees for their opinions, but all my contacts have disappeared under mysterious circumstances.

TIME: 4 hours 20 minutes

YIELD: About 2 quarts

DIETARY: Gluten free, Nondairy, Vegan

DIFFICULTY: Easy

- 8 cups water
- ½ cup fresh mint leaves
- 8 tablespoons good-quality dried black tea leaves (such as Assam or Darjeeling)
- Mint sprigs, to serve
- Lemon wedges, to serve

1. In a large saucepan, bring the water to a boil over high heat. Stir in the fresh mint and dried black tea leaves. Cover and remove from the heat. Let steep for 5 minutes.

2. Strain the tea through a fine-mesh strainer set over a heatproof bowl or container. Let cool to room temperature before transferring to a pitcher and chilling for at least 4 hours.

3. Serve the tea over ice with mint sprigs and lemon wedges to garnish.

ATHENA'S CITRUS SHIELD BOOSTER

Watermelon punched!

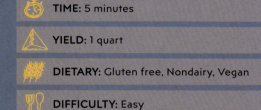

Given Athena's past experiences with robotic entities, it is no surprise that she was initially distrusting of a Loader Bot such as myself. I had hoped explaining my culinary mission would be enough to win her over, but it sadly did little to dissuade her from continuing her assault. Still, with how often I have to face down gunfire, it was a refreshing change of pace to get attacked with a sword and shield instead. I believe I've captured that refreshing sensation in liquid form, minus the inevitable bodily harm.

TIME: 5 minutes
YIELD: 1 quart
DIETARY: Gluten free, Nondairy, Vegan
DIFFICULTY: Easy

- 1 cup watermelon juice
- 1 cup blood orange juice
- ¼ cup fresh lime juice
- ¼ fresh lemon juice
- 1½ cups seltzer or club soda
- Lime wedges, to serve

1. In a pitcher, stir together the watermelon juice, blood orange juice, lime juice, and lemon juice. Top with the seltzer or club soda.
2. Pour over ice and garnish with lime wedges.

MOXXTAIL

Zero proof, but zero complaints.

ACCESSING ECHO LOG. SUBJECT: MOXXI INTERVIEW

"Well, of course I can make you something nonalcoholic, sugar; I aim to please as wide an audience as possible. More than a few Raiders have had to be cut off before they say or do something they'll regret in the morning, but that doesn't mean I won't still take their cash. And what I serve 'em is so good, they don't even notice their drinks have gone soft. Here you go, sweetie. Try this and tell me it doesn't taste like heaven on Pandora."

TIME: 5 minutes

YIELD: 1 mocktail

DIETARY: Gluten free, Nondairy, Vegan

DIFFICULTY: Easy

- ½ cup pomegranate juice
- 1 tablespoon fresh lime juice
- 1 teaspoon rose water
- Seltzer or club soda, for topping
- Lime wedge, to serve

1. Fill a 12-ounce glass with ice. Add the pomegranate juice, lime juice, and rose water. Stir with a cocktail stirrer.
2. Top the glass off with seltzer and garnish with a lime wedge.

MARCUS MULE

Locked and get loaded!

ACCESSING ECHO LOG. SUBJECT: MARCUS KINCAID INTERVIEW

"So . . . you want to hear a recipe, eh? What do I look like, a chef? Bah! I sell ammunition, not ingredients! The only meal I care about is making sure as many bandits as possible eat a bullet, ahaha! Now, for my best customers, maybe I mix up a drink from my private reserve, but I don't see you buying anything, do I? Hmm? Oh, ho ho! Well, if you've got *that much* cash . . . let me see if I've got anything in the back for my new best custom . . . er, I mean, my new best friend!"

TIME: 5 minutes
YIELD: 1 cocktail
DIETARY: Nondairy, Vegan
DIFFICULTY: Easy

- 2 ounces apple pie–flavored moonshine
- ½ ounce lime juice
- Ginger beer, for topping
- Cinnamon stick, to serve

1. Fill a 16- to 20-ounce copper mug with ice. Add the moonshine and lime juice and stir to combine. Top with ginger beer.
2. Grate a little bit of the cinnamon stick over the top of the cocktail, then use the cinnamon stick as garnish by wedging between the ice cubes.

THE ZOMBIE LONG ISLAND OF DR. NED

Undead and loving it!

Sometimes, less is more, and so I'm particularly proud of this iced tea concoction. Dr. Ned's original zombie serum had an eerie green coloration that was described as looking "mighty tasty" by the few remaining locals of Jakobs Cove. Well, with a bit of melon liqueur, I've created something the locals can drink without turning into ravenous flesh-eaters. I do seem to have misplaced the serum sample I was using for comparison, but sometimes risking a few horrible undead monstrosities is the only way to achieve mixological success.

TIME: 5 minutes

YIELD: 1 cocktail

DIETARY: Nondairy, Vegan

DIFFICULTY: Easy

- 1 ounce vodka
- 1 ounce white rum
- 1 ounce blanco tequila
- 1 ounce gin
- 1½ ounces green melon liqueur
- 1 ounce fresh lime juice
- 1 ounce simple syrup
- Cola, for topping
- Lime wedge, to serve

1. Fill a collins glass with ice. Add the vodka, rum, tequila, gin, green melon liqueur, lime juice, and simple syrup. Stir to combine with a cocktail stirrer.
2. Top the glass off with a splash of cola and garnish with a lime wedge.

NOTE: If you don't have ready-made simple syrup, you can make some by bringing two parts sugar and one part water to a boil in a small saucepan. Stir until the sugar is dissolved, let cool, and keep in a sealed container in the fridge for up to 6 months.

136

CALYPSO COOLER

A drink fit for a god-queen

Sometime between their early ECHOnet broadcasts and the formation of their death cult, the Calypso Twins explored several synergistic brand deals to help build their fame. Though I had no personal interest in their custom gun holsters or ECHO device skins, I was drawn to the one drink they cut a promo for. Though the endorsement ended when Tyreen leeched several executives over a contract dispute, this blackberry cooler is still a favorite among holdout Children of the Vault devotees.

TIME: 50 minutes

YIELD: About 2 quarts

DIETARY: Gluten free, Nondairy, Vegan

DIFFICULTY: Easy

- 12 ounces blackberries, divided
- ¼ cup fresh lime juice
- ¼ cup granulated sugar
- 1 bottle crisp white wine, such as sauvignon blanc, chilled
- 3 cups lime-flavored seltzer, ice cold

1. In a large pitcher, combine half the blackberries, the lime juice, and granulated sugar. Lightly mash the blackberries with a muddler or a potato masher. Let sit for 45 minutes, stirring occasionally, until the sugar has dissolved, and the mixture is slightly syrupy.
2. Add the remaining blackberries, followed by the wine and seltzer. Serve in wineglasses, letting some of the whole berries fall into each glass.

THE FIREHAWK

Its Siren song calls to you

Having faced Handsome Jack, the Calypso Twins, and countless Vault monsters, Lilith is arguably the greatest hero Pandora has ever known. As such, she deserves a truly impressive drink to capture her larger-than-life personality. This mix captures not only her spicy personality, it also features a color palette reminiscent of her inimitable Siren powers. Like Lilith herself during a Phasewalk, this drink is sure to disappear fast once you get your first taste.

TIME: 25 minutes

YIELD: 1 cocktail

DIETARY: Nondairy, Vegan

DIFFICULTY: Easy

FOR THE SPICY RASPBERRY-HIBISCUS SIMPLE SYRUP
- 1 cup water
- 2 cups granulated sugar
- 2 cups raspberries (fresh or frozen)
- ½ cup dried hibiscus flowers
- 1 or 2 chile peppers, such as jalapeño, Fresno, or habanero, stemmed and halved

FOR THE COCKTAIL
- 1½ ounces blanco tequila
- 3 ounces orange juice, preferably freshly squeezed
- Orange wheel, to serve
- Fresh raspberry, to serve

TO MAKE THE SPICY RASPBERRY-HIBISCUS SIMPLE SYRUP:

1. In a medium saucepan, combine the water, granulated sugar, raspberries, hibiscus flowers, and chile peppers. Bring to a boil over high heat, stirring until the sugar has dissolved. Remove from the heat, cover, and let steep for 15 to 20 minutes.

2. Strain out the solids and let cool. Store syrup in the fridge in a sealed container for up to 1 month.

TO MAKE THE COCKTAIL:

3. Fill a collins glass with ice. Add the tequila and orange juice, then stir to combine. Slowly pour in ½ ounce of the homemade syrup. It should sink to the bottom to give the appearance of a sunset. Garnish with an orange wheel and a fresh raspberry.

NOTE: This recipe makes about 1½ cups of syrup. This can be made ahead of time and should be stored in the fridge in a sealed container for up to 1 month.

ZANE'S LEMONADE

A Flynt family favorite!

ACCESSING ECHO LOG. SUBJECT: ZANE INTERVIEW

"Yeah, nothin' like a relaxin' drink after a long day out in the field. Trust me, you take out enough bounties and get enough of 'em put on your own head in turn, you learn to enjoy the few peaceful moments you can steal away. 'Course, I always keep my head on a swivel; never know when a family member seeking to settle an ol' blood debt'll show up at your door. When they do, you offer them a nice tall glass of lemonade, work the problem out right then and there. If that's not enough, well, it's what I've got the drone for, isn't it, ha!"

TIME: 25 minutes
YIELD: 2½ quarts
DIETARY: Nondairy, Vegan
DIFFICULTY: Easy

FOR THE LEMONADE
- 3 cups water, divided
- 1 cup granulated sugar
- 1 sprig rosemary
- 1 cup lemon juice

FOR THE COCKTAIL
- 2 cups Irish whiskey, chilled
- 4 cups ginger beer, chilled
- Fresh rosemary, to serve
- Lemon wheels, to serve

TO MAKE THE LEMONADE:

1. In a small saucepan, combine 1 cup of water, 1 cup of granulated sugar, and a rosemary sprig. Bring to a boil over high heat, stirring until the sugar dissolves. Remove from the heat, cover, and let steep for 20 minutes. Strain and chill.

2. In a medium bowl, mix the remaining 2 cups of water, the lemon juice, and homemade rosemary syrup. You should end up with 1 quart of lemonade.

TO MAKE THE COCKTAIL:

3. In a large pitcher or punch bowl, mix the lemonade and whiskey. Carefully stir in the ginger beer. Serve over ice, garnished with rosemary sprigs and lemon wheels.

SCOOTER'S MOTOR OIL SHOOTER

Social lubricant . . . and actual lubricant!

ACCESSING ECHO LOG. SUBJECT: SCOOTER'S PERSONAL LOG

"Yeah, man, I've tasted motor oil! Long nights in the workshop, you get bored and thirsty, right? Shoot, I've tasted coolant, wiper fluid, brake fluid, radiator fluid . . . I had a real fluid period there for a bit, haha! Anyway, I didn't mind the taste none, but Zed kept going on about 'toxicity' and 'deadly consequences,' so I did my best to cut back. Bless my momma, she whipped up a drink that almost tasted like the real thing! It's not as good, but less people seem to end up dead drinkin' it, so . . . ups and downs, y'know?"

TIME: 5 minutes

YIELD: 1 shot

DIETARY: Nondairy, Vegan

DIFFICULTY: Easy

- » 1 ounce herbal liqueur
- » ½ ounce peppermint schnapps
- » ½ ounce cinnamon liqueur
- » ½ ounce coconut rum
- » 1 drop olive oil

1. In a cocktail shaker filled with ice, add the herbal liqueur, peppermint schnapps, cinnamon liqueur, and coconut rum.
2. Shake vigorously for 10 seconds, then strain into a shot glass. Top with the olive oil to create an oil slick on top. Serve immediately.

DIETARY CONSIDERATIONS

RECIPE	PAGE	GLUTEN FREE	NONDAIRY	VEGAN	VEGETARIAN
Angel's Angel Food Cake	106				X
Athena's Citrus Shield Booster	131		X	X	
Axton's "When Life Gives You Lemons" Bars	92				X
Baked Skag Stew	36				
Bandit Chili	47	X			
Brick's Pound Cake	109				X
Calypso Cooler	139	X	X	X	
Claptrap's Birthday Cake for One	101				X
Claptrap's Bits and Bolts	59				
Claptrap's Pizza Party Pizza	49				
Claptrap's Veggie Wrap	25		X	X	
Ellie's Dump Cake	114				X
Ellie's Rusty Wrench Wraps	26				
Eridi-Yum-Yums	105	X		X	
Eridian Éclairs	95				X
Eye(s) of the Destroyer	89				
Firehawk Wings	32		X	X	
Fran's Red Ripple Surprise Frogurt	117	X			X
Gaige's Anarchy Apple Pie	111				X
Grandma Flexington's Fish Pie	40				
Hammerlock and Wainwright's Family Meatloaf	52				
Handsome Flapjacks	12				X
Handsome Mac and Cheese	39				X
Hyperion Finger-Gun Sandwiches	85				
Janey's Springs Salad	86	X	X	X	
Katagawa's Corporate Kenpi	68	X	X	X	
Katagawa's Major Merger Maki	29		X		
Lor's Double Barrel Brew	127	X			X
Marcus Mule	135		X	X	
Maya's Phaselocked French Toast	15				X

RECIPE	PAGE	GLUTEN FREE	NONDAIRY	VEGAN	VEGETARIAN
Meat Bicycle	78				
Mechromancer Muffins	113				X
Mordecai's Incendiary Birdseed	67	X			X
Moxxtail	132	X	X	X	
Mr. Chew's Puppy Chow	60				X
Ned's "Meat" Stew	44		X	X	
Promethean Street Tacos	22	X	X		
Ratch Snax	71	X	X		X
Roland's Crimson Braiders	118				X
Salvador's Seven-Layer Dip	63	X			
Scooter's Motor Oil Shooter	144		X	X	
Skag Jerky	66		X		
Skaghetti and Kriegballs	55				
Strongfork's Greasy Spoon Breakfast	11				
T.K.'s Baha Tacos	19	X			
Tediore's Brisk Ace Tea	128	X	X	X	
Tediore's Farm Fresh Brekki Biggun	16				
The Firehawk	140		X	X	
The Zombie Long Island of Dr. Ned	136		X	X	
Tiny Tina's Beefy Blasters	35	X			
Tiny Tina's Chocolate Chip Cookies	98				X
Tiny Tina's Least-Favorite Oatmeal Raisin Cookies	108				X
Torgue's Anabolic Ammo Bar	76	X	X		X
Torgue's Carnage Cruncher Bar	75	X	X		X
Torgue's Protein Powerhouse Bar	72	X	X	X	
Torgue's Protein Shake	124	X	X	X	
Zane's Beef Stew	21				
Zane's Lemonade	143		X	X	
Zed's Healing Chicken Soup	31	X	X		
Zer0 Calorie Snack Box	82	X			X

DIFFICULTY INDEX

EASY

Athena's Citrus Shield Booster, 131
Bandit Chili, 47
Brick's Pound Cake, 109
Calypso Cooler, 139
Claptrap's Bits and Bolts, 59
Claptrap's Veggie Wrap, 25
Ellie's Dump Cake, 114
Ellie's Rusty Wrench Wraps, 26
Gaige's Anarchy Apple Pie, 111
Grandma Flexington's Fish Pie, 40
Hammerlock and Wainwright's
 Family Meatloaf, 52
Hyperion Finger-Gun Sandwiches, 85
Janey's Springs Salad, 86
Marcus Mule, 135
Meat Bicycle, 78
Mechromancer Muffins, 113
Mordecai's Incendiary Birdseed, 67
Moxxtail, 132
Mr. Chew's Puppy Chow, 60
Ned's "Meat" Stew, 44
Ratch Snax, 71
Salvador's Seven-Layer Dip, 63
Scooter's Motor Oil Shooter, 144
Skaghetti and Kriegballs, 55
T.K.'s Baha Tacos, 19
Tediore's Brisk Ace Tea, 128
Tediore's Farm Fresh Brekki Biggun, 16
The Firehawk, 140
The Zombie Long Island of Dr. Ned, 136
Tiny Tina's Beefy Blasters, 35
Tiny Tina's Chocolate Chip Cookies, 98
Tiny Tina's Least-Favorite
 Oatmeal Raisin Cookies, 108

Torgue's Anabolic Ammo Bar, 76
Torgue's Carnage Cruncher Bar, 75
Torgue's Protein Powerhouse Bar, 72
Torgue's Protein Shake, 124
Zane's Beef Stew, 21
Zane's Lemonade, 143
Zed's Healing Chicken Soup, 31
Zer0 Calorie Snack Box, 82

INTERMEDIATE

Angel's Angel Food Cake, 106
Axton's "When Life Gives You Lemons" Bars, 92
Baked Skag Stew, 36
Claptrap's Birthday Cake for One, 101
Claptrap's Pizza Party Pizza, 49
Eridi-Yum-Yums, 105
Eye(s) of the Destroyer, 89
Firehawk Wings, 32
Fran's Red Ripple Surprise Frogurt, 117
Handsome Flapjacks, 12
Handsome Mac and Cheese, 39
Katagawa's Corporate Kenpi, 68
Lor's Double Barrel Brew, 127
Maya's Phaselocked French Toast, 15
Promethean Street Tacos, 22
Skag Jerky, 66
Strongfork's Greasy Spoon Breakfast, 11

HARD

Eridian Éclairs, 95
Katagawa's Major Merger Maki, 29
Roland's Crimson Braiders, 118

MEASUREMENT CONVERSION CHART

VOLUME

U.S.	METRIC
⅕ teaspoon (tsp)	1 ml
1 teaspoon (tsp)	5 ml
1 tablespoon (tbsp)	15 ml
1 fluid ounce (fl. oz.)	30 ml
⅕ cup	50 ml
¼ cup	60 ml
⅓ cup	80 ml
3.4 fluid ounces	100 ml
½ cup	120 ml
⅔ cup	160 ml
¾ cup	180 ml
1 cup	240 ml
1 pint (2 cups)	480 ml
1 quart (4 cups)	.95 liter

WEIGHT

U.S.	METRIC
0.5 ounce (oz.)	14 grams
1 ounce (oz.)	28 grams
¼ pound (lb.)	113 grams
⅓ pound (lb.)	151 grams
½ pound (lb.)	227 grams
1 pound (lb.)	454 grams

TEMPERATURES

FAHRENHEIT	CELSIUS
200°	93.3°
212°	100°
250°	120°
275°	135°
300°	150°
325°	165°
350°	177°
400°	205°
425°	220°
450°	233°
475°	245°
500°	260°

ABOUT THE AUTHORS

JARRETT MELENDEZ grew up on the mean, deer-infested streets of Bucksport, Maine. A former chef and line cook, Jarrett has worked in restaurants, diners, and bakeries throughout New England and Mexico, and got instruction on Japanese home cooking from some very patient host mothers when he lived in Tokyo and Hiroshima. He's been a professional writer since 2009, but started working as a recipe developer and food writer in 2020. His work has appeared on Bon Appétit, Saveur, Epicurious, and Food52, and he is the author of The Comic Kitchen, an upcoming fully illustrated, comic-style cookbook. When not cooking and writing about food, Jarrett is also an award winning comic book writer. His best known work is *Chef's Kiss* from Oni Press, which won the Alex Award from the American Library Association, along with a GLAAD award nomination for Outstanding Graphic Novel. Jarrett has contributed to the Ringo-nominated *All We Ever Wanted*, *Full Bleed*, *Young Men in Love*, and *Murder Hobo: Chaotic Neutral*. He is currently working on *Tales of the Fungo: The Legend of Cep*, a middle-grade fantasy adventure, to be published by Andrews McMeel. He lives in Massachusetts with his collection of *Monokuro Boo* plush pigs.

JORDAN ALSAQA is a writer based in Seattle, WA. Jordan graduated with a degree in Creative Writing from N.C. State University and has written numerous self-published and work-for-hire comic projects in the years since, including *Raise Hell!*, *Bullet Adventures*, and *Our Sins Are Scarlet*. His fantasy YA graphic novel series *Cooking with Monsters* is published by IDW, and he is currently writing a haunted romance graphic novel scheduled for release in 2027.

PO Box 3088
San Rafael, CA 94912
www.insighteditions.com

 Find us on Facebook: www.facebook.com/InsightEditions
 Follow us on Instagram: @insighteditions

© 2025 Take-Two Interactive Software, Inc. and its subsidiaries. All Rights Reserved. Borderlands, Gearbox, Gearbox Software, 2K, 2K Games and all related titles and logos are trademarks of Take-Two Interactive Software, Inc. and its subsidiaries.

All rights reserved. Published by Insight Editions, San Rafael, California, in 2025.

Marmite® is a registered trademark of Conopco, Inc., a subsidiary of Unilever

No part of this book may be reproduced in any form without written permission from the publisher.

ISBN: 979-8-88663-617-8

Publisher: Raoul Goff
SVP, Group Publisher: Vanessa Lopez
Publishing Director: Mike Degler
VP, Creative: Chrissy Kwasnik
VP, Manufacturing: Alix Nicholaeff
Art Director and Designer: Catherine San Juan
Editor: Sadie Lowry
Editorial Assistant: Jeff Chiarelli
Managing Editor: Nora Milman
Production Manager: Deena Hashem
Strategic Production Planner: Lina s Palma-Temena

Text by Jarrett Melendez and Jordan Alsaqa
Photography by Ted Thomas
Food & Prop Styling by Elena P. Craig

Borderlands Team:

2K Games
Mikayla Jackson – Coordinator, Licensing
Barbara Radziwon – Manager, Licensing
Sean Haran – Head of Partnerships & Licensing

Gearbox Entertainment
Meredith Hershey – Creative Associate
Erica Hollinshead Stead – Director of Franchise Creative Development
Lin Joyce – Managing Director of Narrative
April Johnson – Associate Director of Narrative
Andrew Reiner – Global Creative Executive Officer

Insight Editions, in association with Roots of Peace, will plant two trees for each tree used in the manufacturing of this book. Roots of Peace is an internationally renowned humanitarian organization dedicated to eradicating land mines worldwide and converting war-torn lands into productive farms.

Manufactured in China by Insight Editions

10 9 8 7 6 5 4 3 2 1